The Treasury of Sporting Guns

by
Charles F. Waterman

Special Photography by J. Barry O'Rourke and Robert J. Kligge

A Ridge Press Book ✸ Hamlyn • London • New York • Sydney • Toronto

Editor-in-Chief: Jerry Mason
Editor: Adolph Suehsdorf
Art Director: Harry Brocke
Associate Editor: Marta Hallett
Art Associate: Nancy Mack
Art Production: Doris Mullane
Production Consultant: Arthur Gubernick
Picture Editor: Marion Geisinger

Published 1979 by
The Hamlyn Publishing Group Limited
London • New York • Sydney • Toronto
Astronaut House, Hounslow Road
Feltham, Middlesex
ISBN 0 600 34094 5

Printed in the Netherlands
by Smeets Offset, Weert.

To my wife Debie,
who has put up with all those guns
for all those years.

In compiling this book the author
especially wishes to recognize assistance from
twenty years of The American Rifleman, *publication*
of the National Rifle Association,
and from many of the thirty-two annual issues
of John T. Amber's Gun Digest, *DBI Books,*
Inc., Northfield, Illinois.

The author also wishes to thank
the many tolerant gun owners who have allowed
their treasures to be examined or photographed.
G.T. Herman's Safari Outfitters, Ltd.,
in Ridgefield, Connecticut, and Atlanta Outfitters,
Ltd., in Atlanta, Georgia, were especially
helpful in this regard. Special thanks go to
Leighton Baker, gunsmith, historian, and gun writer,
who deftly separates gun fact from fiction.

Contents

Introduction

For four hundred years sporting firearms have been associated with skill, ingenuity, and art. In many times and places proficiency with guns has been a measure of stature, and their development has long challenged thousands of inventors. The world's artists have worked metal and wood into priceless treasures.

There is no record of the number of guns that have been built, some of them simple tools and others ornate possessions of kings. Sporting guns have long expressed the characters and strong preferences of their owners, and although they may come from an assembly line it can be truthfully said that no two guns are exactly alike.

Often a development from the grim implements of war, the sporting arm has served the needs of survival and sport at the same time, for the ivory hunters of Africa and the beaver trappers of the Rockies have shown in their records that hunting, however mercenary, was yet a form of pleasure for them, challenging and often dangerous.

Hunters have most frequently led the way to far places. The mountain man in his buckskins moved warily through unnamed passes to unknown beaver valleys; in the Himalayas determined hunters sought strange game, hearing more of superstition than of fact; the African bush carried special dangers for travelers with primitive guns; the Plains buffalo hunter became one of the deadliest marksmen of all.

In a later day hunters with more modern rifles probe the Arctic for great white bears and traverse dangerous complications of political boundaries to collect the heavy-horned Asian sheep first reported by Marco Polo. Shooting acquires a social stature far removed from the martial exercise it once was, and the codes of sportsmanship and fair chase are accepted as ritual and tradition. Hunters lead the march of wildlife conservation.

And while connoisseurs of wood scour the forests for just the right walnut for gunstocks from old trees of tortured growth, and metalsmiths inlay figures and inscribe delicate scrolls, the quest for accuracy has never stopped. There is the search for perfect bullets and powder that burns at the exact speed for the bore and bullet, ever pressing for the perfect grouping. Meticulous precisionists bend over rigid benches and ponderous rifle barrels to guide shots into a single scalloped hole hundreds of yards away. International marksmen now aim rifles of futuristic design at tiny targets, engaged in almost hypnotic control of breath, pulse, and nervous system for the perfect letoff.

Ghosts of the great exhibition shooters of another century could stand in awe at modern trap and skeet marksmen who defy the rules for human nerves and list consecutive hits in the thousands, records that cannot be compared with those of Adam Bogardus or W. F. Carver because unknown technicians in gleaming laboratories have produced precise ammunition the nineteenth-century gunners never imagined.

When American market shooting of the 1800s faded with a dearth of game and a protective pattern of laws it was said there would never be enough practice to produce such wing shooters again, but in the twentieth-century sportsmen travel by jet plane to far lands where they can fire cases of shells through hot gun barrels and the flocks of doves, grouse, and waterfowl seem never-ending.

After centuries of desiring guns to fire faster and straighter, sportsmen found that limitations were needed and laws to restrict gun efficiency were made. In some places even semiautomatic rifles were declared illegal. Then a turn to primitive weapons began by factories and shooters, and twentieth-century hunters went forth with the equipment of centuries before. This is partly nostalgia and an attempt to grasp the better parts of a bygone age but it is partly the desire to compete with game on more even terms and a sign that the gunner's frontier legacy is not completely forgotten.

n cw · in ota celelti milh
cempiternam · Qual
qui line fine mmir
men ·

1

The Beginning of Guns

Man, the inventor, was intrigued by projectiles and first extended his range through the throwing stick and the bow. They were the forerunners of sporting guns as catapults were forerunners of cannon. At first, explosive powder was not recognized as a propellant. If its true potential for shaping nations had been realized, its discovery or construction would have been better recorded. As it is, the origins are vague and firearms historians have been unable to pin down an inventor, place, or time. While students of the subject disagree about beginnings they are forced to concede that gunpowder, or something very much like it, probably appeared gradually in widely separated parts of the world.

With her long history of fireworks, China is a logical starting point, but here is the catch that plagues all ancient history of the subject: Did the Middle Kingdom really have gunpowder, or simply a highly flammable substance of similar properties? That unanswerable question insures that definite places and dates will never be established, for it can be asked of any primitive explosive.

Historians often suggest the Arabs as fathers of true gunpowder and the logic of their premise gains in the fact that Arabian culture was flourishing while Europe underwent the Dark Ages. We know the Arabs were chemists and that they served both China and Europe with their science.

But the first name and date to appear are more the result of recording than of invention. The recorder was Friar Roger Bacon of England who set down a formula for gunpowder just before 1250. He is sometimes named as the "discoverer" or "inventor," but undoubtedly more than one person was responsible.

It was no accident that a churchman should report on gunpowder. First, the medieval clergy was most likely to have the time, education, and facilities for experimentation. Early religious leaders used a variety of means to convince the public of their association with the supernatural. "Gun" powder was a dramatic demonstration of the unknown. So although Friar Bacon recorded his observations, it is likely that preceding generations of churchmen had kept powder a secret, except for occasional dramatic displays.

Military uses of powder probably came long before anything resembling a gun. "Greek fire," for example, is believed to have been something closely akin to gunpowder, although accounts of its uses are rather vague. It is believed that Persians who invaded Delphi in 481 B.C. were confronted by an explosion of some sort that must have involved something approximating gunpowder. Another explosion occurred during a Greek battle in 279 B.C., but there were no "guns." These things evidently were tied to the supernatural by observers.

When Hannibal crossed the Alps (218 B.C.), a military operation still studied by the world's soldiers, it is suggested that there was some controlled blasting to get his heavy columns through the passes. A great general was unknowingly close to a great weapon, but explosives had not yet been truly harnessed.

When Bacon, the Franciscan friar, reported on his experiments with powder it is possible some crude cannon were already being used in several parts of the world. The first ones were shaped somewhat like vases and threw missiles resembling crossbow bolts. There were some small, breechloading cannon employed by the Spanish and Majorcans, and similar instruments have been found at Copenhagen. Handguns, at first simply smaller versions of the cannon, appeared around 1350. Before 1500 there were matchlock guns, and that lineage can be traced to sporting arms. Before that, hand-held guns were fired by the application of hot coals or wires to a touch hole — primitive cannon reduced to hand size.

The features that resulted in modern firearms came slowly because they frequently failed in their original forms. For example, breechloading, often regarded as a nineteenth-century development, was actually used with some of the earliest guns, although there was no hinged break action and no smoothly manipulated breechlock. At first the process involved putting the load into a cutout from the barrel and simply plugging the opening with something after the charge was placed. Thus the muzzle-loader was technically more advanced than primitive breechloading.

Once guns were taken up by the military and had their first uses as sporting weapons, including target shooting, the inventor was joined by the artist. Armament had long been decorated by artwork, much of it tied to religion and some of it related to superstition (terms hard to separate at the time). A man who trusted his life to a sword, shield, or battle-ax was unlikely to overlook chances for extra aid from symbolic scrollwork or images. The practices carried over into the early guns used both for hunting and warfare. Religious themes were especially logical, for wars based on religious differences have been as terrible as any. And since hunting was considered closely allied to martial games, hunting weapons were decorated, too. The guns of kings were jewelled treasures.

Some of the simplest developments were longest in coming. For example, the gunstock, seemingly an elementary part of aiming, appeared in incredible shapes for centuries, even after sights were considerably refined. Despite the crossbow, which was finally aimed from the shoulder, gunstocks made false starts in many directions. At first the stock (undoubtedly not called that) was simply an extension of the barrel that could be clamped under the arm. Then there were stocks that rested atop the shoulder and some that were held back against the chest. Others were held to the cheek. Some of the Oriental ones were so strangely shaped that modern students wonder how they *were* held. Pistol stocks evolved faster than those for long guns, following the obvious contours of the hand.

Early firearms fired a variety of projectiles but lead became popular early in the game— easily molded to a bullet shape, heavy enough to retain velocity over long ranges, and soft enough to be controlled by the first rifling. But smoothbore weapons could be used to throw anything that would go into their barrels, including stones or irregular scraps of iron.

Roger Bacon (in portrait) did not invent gunpowder but recorded a formula. Devil himself (below) is depicted as an aid to Black Berthold in experiments with explosives. Hand cannons (opposite page) were used in 14th century. Heavier cannons shown in siege in painting of about 1430 had taken form of later siege and naval guns.

It was the firing mechanism, the machinery that set off the powder charge, which involved inventors for seven hundred years, and other devices had to await its development. The first that could be called a mechanism was the matchlock. It came along with a sort of chamber to be known as a "pan," which held priming powder that, when ignited, would fire the main charge through a small opening. When a movable holder was built to hold a smoldering "match" so that it could be pressed to the charge at will, a "lock" had been invented, however crude.

The first matchlock had a simple serpentine arrangement which pressed the burning cord or match against the powder, holding it in a clamp. Later, the match holder was operated by a real trigger and by late in the fifteenth century some of them worked with a spring. By then, firearms had been accepted by the military and the development of accuracy had begun.

One of the shortcomings was the length of time required to operate the match; a later gunsmith would call it "lock time." In other words, it was necessary for the gun to be held on target for a long time while the match was being applied and the powder ignited. Eventually, lock time was to be measured in milliseconds but the earliest marksmen must have had either a rest or the capability of holding the gun properly aimed for a long period. Such niceties as lock speed were not too important in the terrible business of firing into massed troops but when individual targets were considered the military strategist faced the perpetual choice of aimed fire

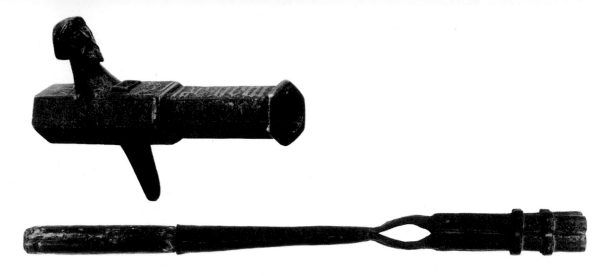

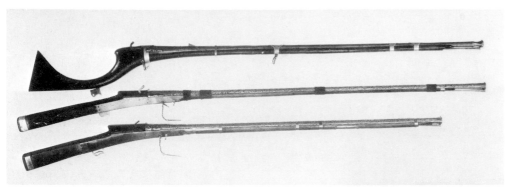

versus saturation fire. Hunters must either locate bunched game or fire with a rest at stationary targets, and some heavy matchlocks required two operators.

Early powders varied greatly in composition, the basic components of saltpeter, sulfur, and charcoal being assembled in a variety of formulas, and often the mixtures did not hold together well, settling so that they separated and became unreliable. An unsatisfactory load in a muzzleloading arm was difficult to remove and a dangerous situation in battle.

But as inventors are wont to do, those of the matchlock days frequently skipped over the badly needed improvements for powder and lock time and turned up complex guns, even repeaters. In some of them several charges were superimposed in the barrel and ignited by individual "matches" on separate serpentines. There were multibarreled guns, another search for firepower, which would be the Holy Grail of firearms inventors until completely automatic weapons were achieved. There were even magazines which reprimed the pan after firing.

Around 1500 the wheellock appeared. It was an extremely complicated mechanism, much more so than the more reliable guns that replaced it. The wheellocks became some of the most prized collector's items because they were likely to be decorated most ornately. Since it was an expensive gun to create, the wheellock was commonly owned by the nobility. The principle was simpler than the construction. A serrated wheel whirled and struck iron pyrites or flint, creating sparks that ignited the pan of priming powder. A spanner or key was car-

ried to wind the spring which drove the wheel. Since the mechanism was far from infallible, some guns were built with an accessory matchlock. The design was to be followed by the less complex and much more efficient flintlock, but ornate wheellocks used by the aristocracy were made until the middle of the eighteenth century—more than two hundred years of production. And the wheellock began to solve the problem of lock time.

Then came a simple but highly efficient mechanism, the flintlock, a design that somewhat overlapped the matchlock and wheellock periods. Such changes were never abrupt. There were flintlocks at about the middle of the sixteenth century and the flintlock period lasted for three centuries, into the nineteenth. By one view, the "flintlock period" never ended at all, for flintlocks have been used through most of the twentieth century by tribes who may never have heard of the atomic age.

The system is simple: a piece of flint held in the jaws of a cock or hammer is struck against steel when a trigger is pulled, releasing the spring-driven cock. The flint causes a spark which ignites powder in a priming pan and the fire flashes through a small hole to the main charge. The snaphaunce was an early form and the steel or frizzen against which the flint struck was manually pulled over the powder before firing. There was a separate cover on the pan to protect it when firing was not imminent. The more advanced and simpler form of flintlock used a frizzen and pan cover in one piece, so that the falling hammer not only struck the flint against the frizzen but also opened the pan cover.

The miquelet, appearing late in the 1500s, was a variation of the flintlock rather than a different system. It carried its spring on the sideplate, generally had longer jaws for a flint clamp, and appeared more complex and even clumsy. It was popular in Spain and was distributed in the Near East. No one will ever know who invented these firing systems, but Leonardo da Vinci made drawings of wheellock and flintlock and there is romantic conjecture that he had a part in both.

Once the flintlock system had been established, gun handles became more practical and accurate hunting weapons were at hand. Rifling was already available and had been found on guns of the matchlock days—even before 1500. Rifling stabilizes a bullet because the spinning tends to minimize the effect of irregularities in form and weight, but these principles were unknown to its first users. The first rifling may have been designed to prevent powder fouling from clogging the bore, or to make it easier to force a tight ball down the barrel. Some early rifling was straight instead of curving.

The supernatural came into consideration, the devil's hand being suspected in the guidance of a spinning ball—somehow. At first the rifle was an instrument of the hunter rather than the soldier, for it was slower to load and military tactics involving tightly massed troops placed small premium on accuracy. Even with the use of a greased patch it took longer to ram a bullet down a rifled barrel. If the rifling did not take hold it was of no use and if the rifling gripped either lead or patch the ramrodding required time-consuming effort.

The detail (opposite) shows a "wick" that furnished fire for the matchlock. The lower guns are a decorated (top) German piece, above (below) a Dutch target model. Battle scene shows French using arquebuses against Florida Indians in the 1560's.

R.Holata Outina.

But although speed was desirable for the hunter, it could be sacrificed for precision. European sportsmen began to use rifles that were far ahead of their time, matching many modern sporting guns in accuracy. It was one of few instances in which the hunter has outstripped the soldier in developments. The accurate European rifle developed into the jaeger, used by German hunters and target shooters, and carried to America as the basis for the Kentucky and the Plains rifles.

Not that the military ignored the new accuracy of compact and powerful rifles. The rifles were used, but as specialized weapons of special units for long-range purposes. The smoothbore musket—simple, inexpensive, and comparatively fast to load—remained the standard weapon for the bulk of Europe's armies.

The jaeger, culmination of the development of European flintlock rifles, appeared gradually, the name coming from a word meaning hunter or marksman. Its immediate ancestor was the wheellock, and although there is no definite date marking its inception, it was the beginning of highly accurate flintlock rifles with a stock shape conducive to com-

19

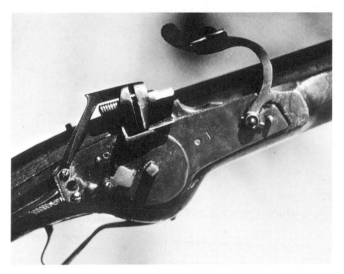

fortable and precise firing. If there must be a date for its birth it should be about 1650. By the eighteenth century it was recognized across Europe as the best hunting rifle.

There was some fairly heavy game in Europe, especially the boar, which could be dangerous. There were and are some larger members of the deer family and there was special need for accuracy. As the jaeger developed at a time when truly high velocity was unknown and impossible, it gained killing power and long-range accuracy from the weight of its bullet. Heavy bullets mean heavy recoil and that could be handled only with properly shaped stocks, stocks which closely resembled modern ones.

A composite of the German jaegers would have a caliber of around .60, a barrel about thirty inches long, and an extended trigger guard that formed a sort of pistol grip. The stock was not excessively bent, the sights were open, and there was a "butt trap" to carry small tools or extra parts (or an extra flint). This small box had a cover of wood, horn, ivory, or bone and occupied the same area of the stock as the "patch box" of the Kentucky rifle. Americans generally used a brass cover. Illustrations of the gun make it appear heavy, but collector Bluford W. Muir states that the average weight was about seven and three-quarter pounds, similar to that of the modern big-game rifle.

German users of the jaeger employed a carrying sling but apparently the sling was not used as an aid to aiming—sling attachments were not designed for such stresses.

One of the chief contributions to marksmanship was the double-set trigger system. One trigger was pulled to "set" the mechanism so that a light touch on the second would fire it. With a single trigger only, the pull would have been quite hard and highly disturbing to careful aim. Double or set triggers continued to be used on high-grade arms until other refined mechanisms made them unnecessary nearly three hundred years later.

Although historians argue about the jaeger's qualities, there are collectors' specimens that can be tested for accuracy against later rifles. While the jaeger will not match the grouping of a twentieth-century target rifle, it will do as well and sometimes better than mass-produced hunting models. It is as accurate as the Kentucky rifles. Recent tests showed a jaeger grouping in two and a quarter inches at one hundred yards, well within the arbitrary limits set for deer rifles in timbered country. There is reason to believe that special jaegers built and tuned for target shooting were capable of even greater accuracy. In some models there were different leaves for the open rear sight to be used at various ranges, the same system found in much later sporting rifles and military guns. The system remained popular in the twentieth century for heavy rifles used at close range against dangerous game.

Many jaegers were highly decorated with delicate engraving and inlays, as well as wood carving. The locks remained fairly standard flint types and in that field the British seemed to be more innovative.

The jaeger came to America with German immigrants, many of whom settled in Pennsyl-

*German breechloading wheellock
(below) had features of
much later guns. Seventeenth-
century over-under wheellock
(opposite) had two separate
"dog heads" and wheels. Such
set triggers and button safety
were in use centuries
later. Over-under design
languished and then came back.
Boar hunters were drawn by
Johannes Stradanus
(1523–1605).*

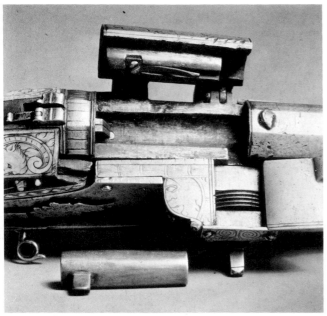

vania, and in time the local gunsmiths produced their own rifle, later to be known as the Kentucky. But for a long while the jaeger pattern was followed in America and it was only a little before the American Revolution that the colonists finally had their own distinctive design. Some students say it was no improvement but simply an attempt to be original.

National pride is so inextricably tied to the "Kentucky rifle," and Americans have so stead-fastly considered themselves a nation of riflemen, that tall yarns of the early frontier have been eagerly accepted as fact. Some of the stories of the early marksmen are beyond the capabilities of the guns used, even if superhuman abilities could have handled the aiming. James Fenimore Cooper's Leatherstocking was larger than life.

But the early American hunter was unique, a product of a really new land, as yet unmapped. He came from immigrants who had used the guns of Mother Europe for food and protection. When the time came for America's hunter to put aside the clumsy matchlock and the delicate wheellock (of which he saw little, anyway) and to use a rifle designed for his own purposes, he made the most of it. And the chroniclers of his adventures have long been excused for their exaggeration.

Many of the first users of the Kentucky rifles were free spirits looking toward the unexplored West, drawn to it inexorably along a thousand Indian and game trails through forests and prairies. They never heard the term, "Kentucky rifle," for it was applied at a later date.

Daniel Boone's Kentucky was farther along the trail west. It was a new country, and when Andrew Jackson's "hunters of Kentucky" fought the British, the words had a good ring to them. Kentucky rifle. The rifle had made a great deal of history long before the Battle of New Orleans.

It is doubtful whether the average American in buckskins could have outshot a much-practiced German who had grown up with target matches. But there was more to a frontier shooter than a steady hand and accurate barrel. There was woodcraft, patience, and continual self-reliance.

The riflemen of America were a minority. Smoothbore muskets were the basic arm of the colonists and they could be used with either ball or shot. They were the tools of protection against unfriendly Indians and the trading stock used with In-

24

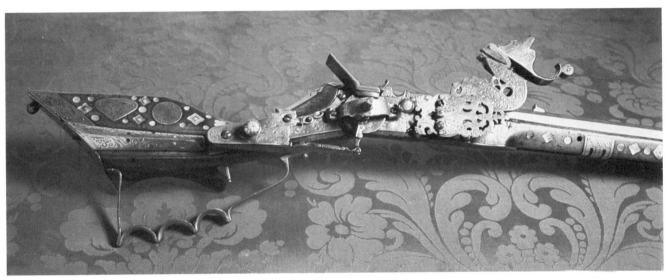

dians who were friendly, at least for the time being. They probably did more to drive off stock-killing wolves than did the rifles.

The blunderbuss, a bell-mouthed gun that fired various kinds of shot, is sometimes shown as a weapon of the Pilgrims. A few undoubtedly found their way to the settlements, although they were primarily a short-range weapon for defense— or personal assault. The bell mouth served only two apparent purposes: to add a fearsome appearance and flash, and to accept hastily poured missiles when loading was urgent. It was no squirrel gun.

Not only is the development of the Kentucky rifle a bit mysterious but the designers' objectives are vague and general statements about its merit tend to be ambiguous. It grew from the jaeger and from the hands of gunsmiths who knew its European ancestors, but was it really an improvement or merely expression of a form of folk art?

Poetic reference to the Kentucky's graceful appearance is well founded but it is improperly described as a replacement for a heavy, awkward, inaccurate, and impractical jaeger rifle. The first Pennsylvanians were nearly the exact image of the jaeger. Most of them were plain, sturdy guns and most early Kentuckys were relatively undecorated. The decoration tended to become flamboyant and overdone late in the Kentucky's career.

The essential differences from the jaegers were longer barrels, a very different stock formation, and a somewhat smaller caliber. As to actual weight, the American gun was lighter only in some cases; it was almost invariably longer.

The lighter caliber is unquestioned but the difference was not as much as is commonly stated. Flat statements about the small caliber of the

American rifle are probably influenced by the occasional true squirrel rifle with a caliber of only .32 to .38. The average caliber seems to have been more nearly .45 or a little larger, and many bores were "freshened" to a larger size as the rifling wore. This encourages the heretical statement that the rather strangely shaped Kentucky stock wasn't practical for heavy recoil.

The calibers, compared to the jaeger's average of nearly .60, were satisfactory for nearly all eastern game, and the smaller balls took up little space, were easy to carry, and used a minimum of lead over a rather flat trajectory. Remember, the pioneer hunter moved his moccasins for long distances.

The new rifle was long, very long, with most barrels well over forty inches, about a foot longer than the jaeger's. The reasons given for this length is added sighting radius, more efficient powder burning, and less noise. Later generations of hunters made a point of preferring short guns for use in heavy cover, and since the eastern rifleman was primarily a timber stalker, later authorities are surprised at his willingness to carry five feet of rifle on tortuous game trails.

The Kentucky rifle was not carried much with a sling and it seems a poor choice for horseback use, but the long barrel may well have been something of a status symbol, identifying the user as one of the woodsman's loose brotherhood. A finely shaved translucent powder container made of natural horn was part of the costume, as well as a practical loading aid.

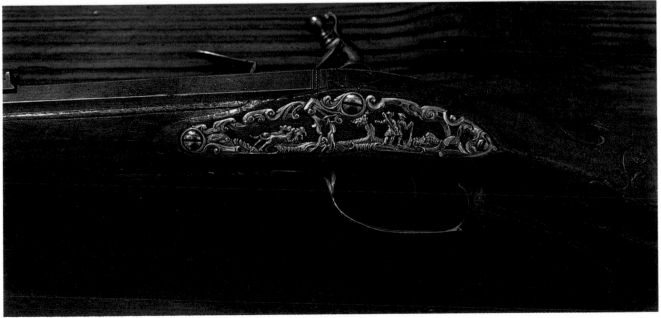

Sighting equipment was fairly simple, generally a notch rear sight and a blade front, with the former sometimes adjustable for windage through some effort. Undoubtedly many of the rifle's users "held off" rather than making any kind of sight change, and the term "Kentucky windage" is still used by shooters who know their rifles are not shooting exactly where the sights indicate.

But the stock, full length in the classic specimen, might be the most distinguishing feature. It generally had a great deal of drop—that is, the comb of the stock was well below the line of sight and slanted steeply downward. It was often made of curly maple or other colorful wood and the buttplate was curved to fit the shoulder, more curve than was found in the jaeger. Deeply curved buttplates were found on many hunting rifles into the twentieth century, but later stock combs were straighter. Users of some Kentucky rifles could aim with their heads erect.

It is doubtful that many of the first American rifle builders started out as full-time gunsmiths, most of them making other things as well, and it must be remembered that a gunmaker had to construct most of his own tools for the purpose. During the early days of American guns there was little specialization, each gunsmith beginning with a piece of wood and some pieces of metal. As the industry developed, there was a system of apprenticeship much like that of Europe. The student's period of service was about seven years at first, somewhat less later on, as the various gun parts began to come from specialized makers. The early apprentice was a servant of the gunsmith and was likely to be indentured.

Apparently the trade was never as formal as that of Europe, where the "graduating" apprentice traditionally produced a showpiece gun as a demonstration of his skill. A great many colonists were engaged in gunmaking, and in a span of two hundred years it has been estimated that there were more than six thousand people in the business. Many of them were blacksmiths, shoeing horses as well as shaping rifling.

Some locks were made in America but more of them came from England. Historians are confused by the fact that some gunmakers put their names on locks made by someone else. Stocks and barrels were produced in the frontier shops. Barrels were regularly formed from strips of iron pounded and welded about mandrels, and the rifling was cut with hand-operated machinery. There were some brass barrels and it is assumed the bore was drilled through those, since the mandrel system does not seem adaptable to brass.

Although Pennsylvania, especially the Lancaster area, is regarded the home of rifle making, there were builders in all the other colonies. Pennsylvania had so many gunsmiths that the rifleman's tradition remained there and the state still produces more than her share of fine marksmen.

Small and relatively inexpensive but critical to the operation of early rifles were the flints. There were some efforts at producing them in America, but nearly all came from England, where the trade of "flint knapping," or shaping, reached its

Breechloading flintlock was truly before its time. Ferguson's rifle, used by some British units in the American Revolution, died with its inventor on King's Mountain. Army politics is blamed for loss of a highly practical weapon. One of the original (far right) military models. Breech mechanism and its threaded opening appears in detail (right).

highest form and where the best flint material always has been quarried. A flint was good for fifty to sixty firings and was gripped in the hammer by a clamp padded by leather or lead. When shooters of the late twentieth century returned to primitive weapons, they supported a small but active English flint industry. When thousands of old flintlocks were converted to the more modern and efficient percussion system there were a few staunch frontiersmen who said makeshift flints could be rigged in an emergency but that a hunter could run out of caps, so they clung to the old way.

Although formal shooting matches with guns had been popular in Europe since about 1400, competitions in America had much less tradition and were not well chronicled until after 1800. Marksmanship was a matter of pride but shooters were too scattered, the frontiers changed too rapidly, and there were more serious matters to be confronted. Thus, shooting matches were informal.

At the time of the Revolution the prowess of the buckskin rifleman was still surprising to most colonists, and the frontier units that joined the rebelling Continentals amazed the citizenry with feats of accuracy, suggesting that the coonskin-cap people were showmen as well as marksmen.

Riflemen, using sniping tactics learned from the Indians, performed demoralizing feats during the French and Indian wars, but it was a hundred years before rifled arms took over the infantry. The Revolution was fought primarily with smoothbore muskets, although in special situations the backwoods rifleman turned the tide, picking off British

officers from great distances. American history, colored by frontier tradition, glows with feats of the rifle-bearing backwoodsman, but there was some similar sharpshooting from a seldom-mentioned source—the Hessians.

The Germans were mercenary troops paid for by the British. Actually, they were units rented by the Crown. Some were scrapings of the manpower barrel and they lacked the drive of a personal cause, but there were some specially chosen units armed with the ubiquitous jaeger. They appeared with terrifying efficiency from time to time and the Virginia infantry was shaken when its personnel fell before long-range German marksmen at Yorktown.

And although we deal with the sporting aspects of firearms, their development is tied to the military, for war is a powerful incentive to invention and military subsidy makes possible the rapid perfection of systems. Why was the rifle so slow in reaching the rank and file of the world's armies?

There were two reasons, one obvious to anyone who understands muzzleloading rifles and one a bit incredible to a twentieth-century man who has lived in a foxhole. The first reason was that a rifled barrel was dangerously slow to load. When tight-fitting balls were forced down without a greased patch it was generally necessary to use a mallet with the ramrod, and even with the patch the ramming was time-consuming. The slowness made it impossible for rifle infantry to confront massed muskets at short range, and early riflemen were not deployed to stop bayonet charges. Evidently, most American

riflemen of the revolutionary period did not have bayonets and at close combat range marksmanship becomes equally sketchy, even from accurate weapons. Soldiers are afraid, nearly always afraid.

The second reason for slow acceptance of the rifle is more complex. Battle still clung to tradition to some extent and to codes carried down from the days of jousting knights. Generals still had strong feelings about what was fair and what was not. Shooting an enemy from long range was not quite sporting and, strangely, it was considered poor leadership for a high-ranking officer to hide from gunfire. So the long-range rifleman was not yet accepted in traditional circles. Even in the age of modern warfare there has been at least one case during World War II when General Douglas MacArthur declined to take cover from a Japanese sniper, although his staff followed no such code.

The Ferguson rifle, which died in 1780 with its Scottish inventor, Lt. Col. Patrick Ferguson, atop King's Mountain, was one of several false starts that might have advanced firearms dramatically. Ferguson, a career officer in the British army, designed a breechloader, not the first but a highly practical one with rugged and simple features.

Ferguson's rifle, though used effectively by small units of the British army, was evidently held back by army politics. The principle was a fast, coarse-threaded screw that was turned from beneath by the trigger guard and which served as a plug to the rifle's breech. When retracted it was possible to drop in a ball which rolled forward to the front of a chamber as the muzzle was lowered. Powder was dumped into the hole left by the retracted

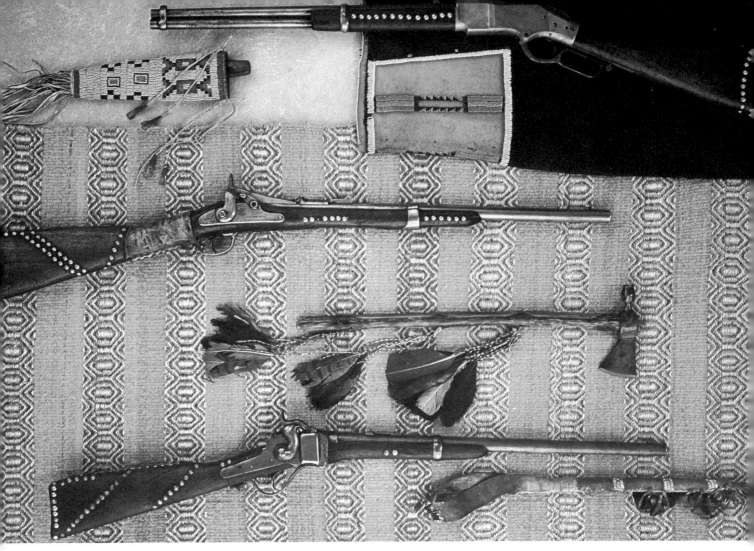

screw, the screw breech was closed, and a conventional flintlock was used for firing. In a 1776 demonstration, Ferguson showed King George III that he could fire seven accurate shots a minute.

There is what appears to be an authentic story related by Ferguson: Having an opportunity to kill George Washington during the Brandywine-Philadelphia campaign, Ferguson declined to shoot when a mounted Washington refused his commands to stop. Washington, Ferguson said, rode away in unhurried dignity. There was apparently less chivalry involved when Ferguson was shot down as he and his sharpshooters tried to defend King's Mountain against concealed colonial marksmen.

Early breechloaders often employed metal cartridges but the cases were not disposable and might be termed removable breech sections instead. Practical cartridge arms awaited the invention of advanced forms of detonation, well into the nineteenth century.

Flintlock fowling pieces, generally double-barreled, were owned by wealthy people in both Europe and America but the finely built fowler was best known in Britain, which became the traditional home of the best in shotguns.

The outstanding example of early flintlock shotguns is a richly figured, lightweight fowler made for Louis XIII of France in 1615 when he was fourteen years old. It was built by Pierre Le Bourgeoys of Lisieux, France, and was recently bought by the Metropolitan Museum of Art in New York for $300,000.

At first, shotguns were primarily for the collection of small game for the table. Sports hunting as practiced by the nobility was confined mainly to larger game, except where falcons and hounds were concerned. Hunting was something of a martial pastime and early hunting expeditions by royalty employed military tactics and equipment. It was natural that development of military and big-game weapons

Indians used brass tacks for decoration of their guns. These 19th-century models are (from top) an 1866 Winchester carbine, breechloading Springfield with "trapdoor," and 50-caliber Sharps as used by professional buffalo hunters. Crow leggings, scalping knife, pipe tomahawk and ceremonial rattle complete display on Indian's decorated blanket.

would receive more attention, but wingshooting gradually took a place as an amusement of the wealthy. The Pilgrims used what was called a "long fowler" and at that time flintlock shotguns took two directions.

To begin with, heavy matchlock smoothbores had been used to kill massed birds; then there were lighter guns for sports hunting. In the 1600s shotguns were made lighter for walking wingshooters and much longer and heavier for pot shooting. The big long fowlers might be as much as eight feet long and they evolved into punt guns that served commercial shooters of later generations. Most of the long fowlers were fired from rests and blinds.

Although the American rifle has been publicized much more than the shotgun, and there were evidently more rifles, shotguns were built in the colonies along with the Kentucky, and there was a definite relationship in the designs. American gunsmiths used components from both England and Germany before making their own in the eighteenth century. There was never a time after Pilgrim days when Americans did not have good shotguns, although they were seldom as ornate as those of the European nobility. As with the Kentucky rifle, the American shotgun was practical but generally lacked the fine artistry of Europe.

If it was not as graceful as a European fowler, the smoothbore musket still served with shot almost as well as with ball and was one of the most versatile of all guns. It was large enough in caliber to throw considerable shot in some sort of a pattern,

and it would hurl other odds and ends as well. At close range it was good enough for large game, although its accuracy limit for that purpose was somewhere around fifty yards. Filled with shot it was good for squirrels, ducks, or grouse, and it was relatively inexpensive. In time of war it could wear a bayonet and be at home in the lines.

For every fine fowling piece or super-accurate Pennsylvania rifle there have been dozens of plain weapons, many of obscure manufacture, that have found their way into the hands of people who regarded them as tools. By 1650 the American Indians were being supplied with guns as the Dutch traded freely with them for furs. The British had passed on a few guns to the Mohawks earlier in the century. Once the Indian appetite for firearms had been whetted, the fur trade became tremendously profitable.

There could never be any accounting of the numbers of matchlocks, snaphaunces, and then standard flintlocks that went to the red men, for Indian trade was ever a quasi-legal thing and there were all sorts of laws against supplying "savages" with firearms. The guns were made in many parts of Europe, and they varied greatly in type at first, though rather definite Indian requirements began to emerge and the "trade gun" eventually took an established pattern.

The Indian wanted a short, handy gun and the "Indian trade fusil" filled those requirements. There were never enough guns to fully satisfy the Indians but by 1750 there were guns in the hands of tribes over the entire continent, except for some

33

Muskets of the American Revolution are (top to bottom) Charleville, Brown Bess, American Brown Bess, and German Brown Bess. Other typical muskets (right) as well as Queen Anne Musket, c. 1690 (below, right) and early Brown Bess, c. 1725–60 (below, left).

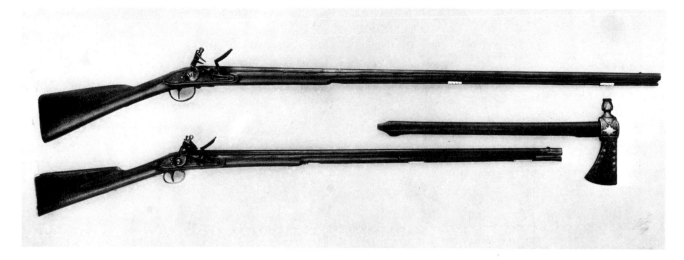

in the far Northwest. Despite pious pronouncements and unenforced laws restricting the use of guns, every nation that attempted to colonize America had provided guns for them.

A preferred Indian gun, known as the Northwest gun, Hudson's Bay "fuke," or Mackinaw gun, was a light smoothbore, and although its short range may have given rise to early ridicule of Indian marksmanship, the trade gun was ideal for tepee living and travel by canoe and horse. The Indian lived with his gun as he had lived with his bow, and his woodcraft more than made up for short range. As to the convenience of a short barrel, the "horse Indians" of the nineteenth century sometimes cut off their barrels to little more than pistol length and used such bellowing, fire-breathing hybrids in buffalo running.

By the nineteenth century the Indian trade gun had one nearly universal feature—it was decorated with a metal dragon. The scaled figure, generally appearing on the lock plate, had no significance known to later researchers but similar animals had been embellishing European armament for years, and after the dragon appeared on a few shipments of Indian guns it began to be accepted as a mark of authenticity, although provided by makers from all over the world. The Indians insisted on it.

The Hudson's Bay fuke was typical of the guns traded to Indians, and like other smoothbores it was of around .66 caliber—about 16 gauge, so it could serve as a shotgun. There was one disadvantage to the shotgun: true lead shot could not be molded by hand as could the large balls, but other

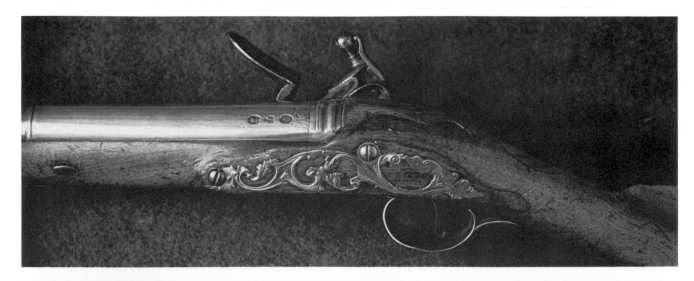

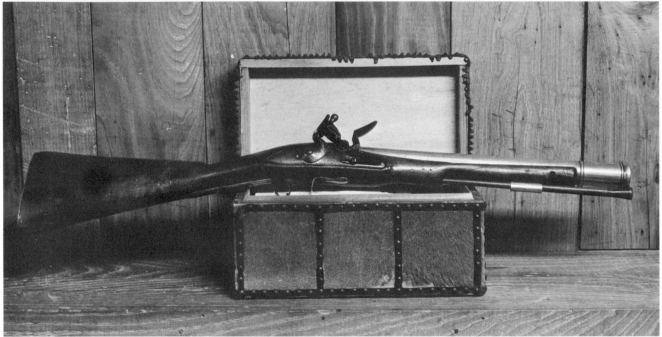

objects such as pebbles could be substituted in an emergency. As the Indian trade advanced into the nineteenth century many trade guns were made in the United States, American laws concerning Indian trade still being flagrantly ignored.

In his day and in regularly revived periods of popularity since, the long rifleman was a folk hero, America's first. He was showman as well as hunter. The coonskin cap, frequently with the tail left on as decoration, the fringed and sometimes beaded buckskin clothing, the often-decorated rifle with its figured stock, and the long knife set him apart from ordinary townspeople and farmers. With only slight regional differences, he lived from the

southern colonies to Hudson's Bay, where he spoke French.

The long rifle was restless and it turned westward, sometimes to follow the fur trade and sometimes to establish new frontiers as did Boone in Kentucky, but ever it pointed farther west. The French fur traders, their exploits recorded less well than those of the Americans, had gone far toward the Pacific and seen the Rockies first. Then Lewis and Clark went farthest of all, and they recorded their passage. They met the great humpbacked bear and the seas of buffalo, and hunting would never be quite the same. The long rifleman followed hard on the trail of Lewis and Clark and he wanted a different firearm, one with some important changes. He became a "plainsman" and a "mountain man." Requirements were about the same.

In the East the hunter had moved mainly on foot. He had studied the trails of whitetail deer that came down from high bedding grounds to feed and returned at dawn, and he had covered the return trail in looping investigations, knowing his quarry would be bedded downwind from its backtrail. And when he had completed the laborious stalking he would come upon his game at fairly close range and the long-barreled rifle would bark sharply, but not loudly enough to reach too many curious ears.

When he hunted the squirrels of the uncut hardwood canopies he could sit for an interminable time until an inquiring quarry showed a beady-eyed head on a high limb. And he learned the wild turkey's language for both fall and spring, his dull-colored buckskins absorbed by the hues of a tree trunk. Although he sometimes fought Indians he was proud of his acceptance of many of their ways.

In the marshy lowlands of the northeastern lakes and rivers he could find the ponderous moose, or call him with a birchbark funnel. He could stalk silently in a birchbark canoe, made as the Indians had made it for centuries, the largest of all deer that probed the lake bottom for vegetation. He would shoot the moose at close range and follow its blood trail if it were not killed immediately. And in winter the process was simplified because trailing was easier and sometimes snow restricted game movements. He knew about snowshoes and how to make camp with only a wisp of fire and a thread of smoke.

But when the woodsman went west to the enormous plains and the great mountains he met the buffalo and the grizzly. The buffalo was food and shelter but it was thicker-shouldered than the moose. He was likely to find it in the open where a long shot was necessary and tracking was complicated since the quarry could watch its backtrail.

The grizzly, the first American animal that directly opposed man's exploration, was a different challenge. The wolf and the cougar preyed on man's livestock and ate his poultry, and the fox stole from him, but the grizzly stood in his way and challenged his passage. The grizzly might hunt the hunter and it had to be stopped. A wound was not enough. The grizzly had to be killed or broken down, for dying grizzlies did not always die alone.

And the western traveler went on horseback. He needed a new gun. He went to the gunsmiths and told them his troubles and the Plains rifle or the mountain rifle was the result.

The rifle that developed was at first a modification of the Kentucky-Pennsylvania in larger caliber, but there were other needs. The Kentucky's barrel was too long and its graceful stock was too fragile for a fall from horseback, almost certain to occur sooner or later. And the heavier recoil necessitated a blockier stock to absorb the shock. With the heavy barrel there was no wish for a full-length stock, so there was a half-stock. And shiny decorations might be sunlit signals to unwelcome eyes, so the Plains rifle was plain—and very, very similar to the jaeger rifle of Europe, from which the Kentucky had evolved.

2

Age of Invention

Recorded history of the American hunting adventure tends to concentrate on brief periods of time such as the era of the mountain man, the buffalo hunter, and the market shotgunner. Each form of hunting had its separate peak years, even though there was a great deal of chronological overlap.

The mountain man's heyday was short. If his time can be said to have begun with the Lewis and Clark expedition in 1804, it was virtually at an end by 1840. He had not trapped out all of the beaver, but when other materials became more popular than beaver fur for society's tall hats the true mountain man's purpose disappeared.

The mountain man's need for a grizzly stopper and a buffalo killer brought changes in firearms before flintlock gave way to percussion. However, the completely developed Plains rifle was not recognized until about 1830. By then percussion was accepted and efficient, although the military stayed with flintlocks.

Percussion arms were the true gateway to modern cartridges, although the caplock had a short career compared to the flint. The caplock, with its enclosed explosive, was firmly established shortly after 1830 and was losing its general popularity by the end of the Civil War.

It began with explosive fulminates, and Alexander John Forsyth, a Scottish clergyman, acquired an English patent and designed a variety of locks to employ them. According to some historians, he reported that the flashing pan of his flintlock frightened birds, so that they could evade the charge—a rather incredible complaint about lock time. The "scent bottle" lock was one of his more distinctive creations. The detonating fulminate was fed into a firing tube when the metal "bottle" was rotated on a pin fastened beside the breech. When the bottle was righted, a hammer would drive the firing pin through it into the explosive. After that there was a variety of schemes from a variety of inventors utilizing explosive material in all sorts of pills, tapes, pellets, and patches.

These inventions did not have time for wide use before the true percussion cap appeared. It was developed by many at about the same time, but is often considered the invention of Joshua Shaw of Lincolnshire, who emigrated to America in 1814 and had the cap in efficient form by 1817. Some plainsmen, mountain men, and pioneer settlers accepted the cap promptly. Others stuck with the flintlock for many years. Later, "cap-and-ball" was spoken almost as a single word.

A study of the first men who pushed forth to the Rocky Mountain beaver streams from the eastern United States leaves the haunting thought that they were in the invisible footsteps of even earlier beaver seekers, the French wanderers who had come from eastern Canada by canoe, horse, and moccasin, had accepted Indian ways, and seen the Rockies long before Lewis and Clark put them on the first reliable maps. While later travels of mountain men from St. Louis were often unrecorded, and even secret, those of the French hunters, trappers, and traders are only shadowy adventures with little to separate fact from fantasy. Many of the French were absorbed into Indian tribes.

Since the era lasted only thirty-five years, it would have been possible for a single trapper to have lived from the beginning to the end of the true "mountain man" era. Few if any did, at least while trapping was a full-time career. The mortality rate was high, as it must be for men cut off from society. Grizzly bears, hostile Indians, and fur thieves caused many deaths, but less colorful perils of disease, accident, starvation, and freezing probably left more unmarked graves and unburied bones. There were long lists of men "never seen again."

The very nature of beaver trapping encouraged penetration into unknown territory. One of the romantic aspects of the mountain man's existence was his annual appearance at the "rendezvous," a meeting place for selling furs and securing supplies. Often he came from an unnamed valley with an unnamed river, and when he left the rendezvous, possibly having drunk or gambled away his year's income, he would return to a rude cabin or campsite by following natural landmarks. Or he would seek new trapping grounds farther into the unknown. He might be unable to make or follow a map. It was for such individualists, rebels, outcasts, and heroes, that the Plains rifles were made.

The Plains, or mountain, rifle was accurate and it threw a heavy round ball, its range limited more by sighting equipment than by actual killing power. A caliber of .50 was typical and it could serve on large game out to two hundred yards for a good marksman, with little "Kentucky windage" necessary for the first one hundred and fifty. Like the Kentuckys it often had double-set triggers to give a delicate letoff. The brass front sight that had gleamed so distinctly in shadowed eastern forests was generally abandoned for something with less reflection.

The rifling was gradual and shallow, making it extremely tolerant of charges—an essential qualification for a gun to be mistreated and used under adverse conditions. A good rifle of the type could handle up to more than 200 grains of black powder, but was satisfactory with much lighter loads for ordinary shooting.

A man intending to spend a year or more (even a short lifetime) in the unknown wilderness generally took considerable powder and lead with him. Just how much he would carry in lead bars or molded balls was a personal matter. It has been suggested that one hundred pounds of lead was not uncommon, but that would provide more than three thousand bullets for the average rifle, probably more than most trappers would need. In any event, the powder and lead for a pair of travelers would make up a large share of a packhorse's load. Some ammunition was carried as prepared cartridges—actually powder and ball in a single package without a detonator.

The rifles generally weighed nearly ten pounds and artists of the time usually depicted them being carried across the rider's lap, balanced across the saddle itself, or in the crook of his arm. The use of slings or carrying straps is very seldom depicted in western art, except when used by the military.

In The Trapper's Last Shot
William Ranney depicts
colorful buckskin garb as was
adopted by early mountain men.
A double-barreled German
percussion gun (below, right)
of about 1840 employs center-
hung hammers and single
trigger, both of which were
to appear as modern devices
many years later. Dragon was
traditional decoration of time.

Since the carrying strap had been employed for centuries in Europe and elsewhere it is strange that a man traveling for weeks on end would carry a ten-pound rifle in his hands, but collectors' samples have few provisions for slings.

Many drawings and paintings show both whites and Indians of the muzzleloading days carrying their guns in protective cases, usually of leather and with fringes (which carry off rain water), but no true saddle scabbards are shown, even though some of the guns were short enough to be carried.

Through history, trade names of various guns have frequently been used to indicate an entire type. At a later date, "Winchester" came to mean "repeating rifle," even in some law books, and "Greener" meant "shotgun," although the name comes from a single British manufacturer. Thus, "Hawken" was sometimes used to indicate the Plains rifle, simply because some of the best and most famous of them were made by the Hawken brothers. They were Jacob and Samuel, sons of Henry Hawkins, who was a Maryland gunsmith, and they achieved their fame in St. Louis where they first altered typical Kentuckys for Plains use and then built their own rifles. They changed their name to the old German spelling.

St. Louis was the staging point for the unknown frontier, first for mountain men and then for home seekers and their wagon trains. The Missouri River was an avenue of traffic to the Northwest, as dusty trails were avenues toward the Southwest.

The Hawken rifle was good and it was chosen by General William H. Ashley, who headed the Rocky Mountain Fur Company and set up the highly profitable (for the buyers) rendezvous system for the trappers. There were many other makers who produced rifles of the same type, some of them of excellent quality. Users of the Plains rifles included such famous names of history as Kit Carson, Jim Bridger, and Joseph L. Meek.

The beaver trapper's rifle was mainly for protection and for collecting meat, but since later woodsmen ambushed working beaver, there probably was more beaver shooting than has been reported. The steel trap was the backbone of the fur business. However, Indians sometimes killed beaver families in their houses, so there were undoubtedly white hunters who did the same thing.

The Plains rifle remained plain in appearance, and its mechanism was simple. A frontiersman could carry a spare lock for it with fair assurance that he would not need a gunsmith for a long while. He had a bullet pouch, a container for caps or flints, and a powder horn. When he adopted the percussion cap the muzzleloader became more weatherproof.

As if to confuse historians of the "era" of the Plains rifle, there remained frontiersmen who used something entirely different, generally the smoothbore. A shotgun could handle a heavy ball when necessary and do a good job on small game with shot, and it was natural that some detractor should give it the name of "squaw gun."

Part sport, part livelihood, and part exhibitionism, the game of "buffalo running" was often played with short smoothbores by both Indians

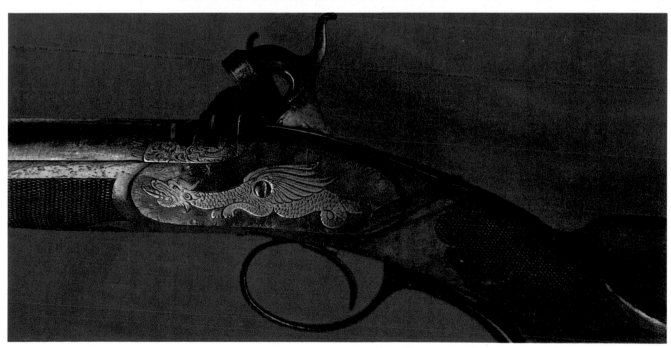

and whites. A century before the peak of the buffalo-hide trade there were buffalo runners. Half a century before the bison's near destruction, firearms were used at close range the way spears and arrows had been used ever since the Indians acquired the Spaniards' horses.

It was some time after the percussion cap became common that Rudolph Friederich Kurz, western traveler and writer, described buffalo running in the 1850s. He said the favorite gun was a flintlock, because of its convenience. The hunter rode his horse alongside the game and fired forward into the heart-lung area at a distance of a few feet. He carried round balls in his mouth and after a shot he poured powder into his left palm from his horn, holding the stopper in his teeth and carrying the gun "close within the bend of his left arm." Then, closing the powder horn, he would take the gun in his right hand, holding it vertical and pouring the powder down the warm barrel.

The rest of the loading process was indeed a trick. By giving the gun a "sidelong thrust" with his left hand the rider would shake powder into the touchpan. Then the bullet would be dropped

Shooting match (opposite, top) was popular holiday sport and frequently involved living targets, usually turkeys. Scent bottle locks on double-barreled wildfowler (below, left) were invented by Rev. Alexander John Forsyth. Multi-groove rifling (left) is shown in views of large bore Huhnstock and Horneffer jaegers.

from his mouth into the barrel. Wet with saliva, it stuck to the powder and fouling.

All of this was done on the back of a galloping horse, hopefully trained to the buffalo chase, and while it may not have been too common a process it is described so minutely that it achieves an authentic ring. In one of his paintings Frederic Remington depicts "mouth loading."

Such a loosely charged gun would not have been accurate enough for long shots. There are paintings of long muzzleloading rifles or middle-length Plains rifles being loaded from a standing horse with the buttstock placed in a stirrup to brace the gun against the thrust of the ramrod. Whether a muzzleloading rifle with a patched ball could be loaded efficiently without stopping the horse remains a question, but a lifetime of gun handling produces surprising dexterity in special situations.

Whether equipped with rifle or smoothbore, the frontier wanderer's problem was one of firepower. As a backup gun he often carried a muzzleloading pistol or a percussion revolver, with a heavy knife as his last resort. The revolving cylinder became the most efficient of repeating mechanisms, but it was never as successful with rifles and shotguns as it was with pistols. Cylinder guns could not stand up under the heavy charges that went into ten-pound singleshot rifles.

But the revolving cylinder was easy to operate once percussion caps became practical. It had been unsatisfactory when tried with flintlocks. The firing system of the percussion cap is very simple: a nipple accepts the cap at the end of a short flash tube extending to the powder charge. When the hammer explodes the cap there is a hot flame more efficient than spark from a flint. With a cylinder gun, all the chambers can be loaded and capped, each chamber being turned under the hammer and into contact with the barrel before firing. With easily removed cylinders the shooter can carry loaded spares and insert them when needed.

The first problems were obvious. To keep it within reasonable size, the cylinder was sometimes too weak for an overload and could rupture. Alignment with the barrel at the time of firing was critical, and before metallic cartridges there were numerous accidents in which one fired chamber set off others. Thus, the user of percussion repeaters often sacrificed heavy charges for rapid fire. Best known of the early revolving long arms were the Colt Paterson rifles. Some other revolving mechanisms employed turret-shaped or "flat" cylinders revolving on a vertical axis, but none of that type was ever capable of handling heavy loads. Some revolving chambers were turned by manipulating the hammer, as with later single-action handguns; others worked with various types of levers.

From the time of the first percussion guns until 1900 there were hundreds of inventors with some highly impractical firearms gadgetry, but the trend was toward improvement of loading speed and convenience. Europe and America kept fairly well abreast in arms development with England taking an early lead in shotguns. The modernization of guns did not move rapidly in Asia, the matchlock remaining the basic firearm in India and Japan. Pro-

fuse decoration, sometimes applied to guns never intended for use, was characteristic of the Orient. In Africa, Europeans were beginning to use some enormous smoothbores on the world's largest game, and the British were intrigued by Indian hunting. It was the British sportsman who became best known as a world traveler, and hunting was the logical sport for energetic young army officers in strange lands a long way from home.

At the time, the American frontier caught the focus of world attention and Westerners continued their "love affair with guns," a marriage of necessity. There were a great many American firearms inventions that were hard to prove out because the stakes were too high in frontier life. There was reluctance to practice new contrivances on irate grizzlies, unfriendly Indians, and the winter's meat. So the men who needed guns most held back their development through insistence on simplicity. There have been stories of percussion guns being converted to flintlocks at a time when most alterations were the other way around. Then, too, the frontier gun might be needed for heavy game and hardly any of the new inventions was strong enough to withstand a charge consisting of a .60-caliber ball and enough black powder to conceal it.

The things most needed were self-contained weatherproof cartridges and breechloading and repeating systems. Breechloaders and repeaters, though they had been made for centuries, were not practical for rough use. The revolving cylinder seemed the most logical repeater, but had special weaknesses in shoulder guns.

In 1848 Walter Hunt of New York City patented a conical lead bullet with a cavity in its base covered by a disc which had a hole to admit flame for firing. The bullet, named the Rocket Ball, was used in a repeating rifle which proved too fragile for success. The gun was a direct ancestor of the Winchester repeating rifles.

Smith & Wesson came up with a copper rimfire .22 short cartridge in 1857, and in ensuing years some seventy-five different rimfire cartridges were produced. Although the rimfire system is ideal for very small calibers it was not quite satisfactory with larger ones and centerfire ammunition eventually took over when more power was needed.

It would still be called "black powder" by modern gunners but the propellant had been greatly improved by mid-century. The very first powder was dustlike and unreliable and was hard to keep mixed. Then the fine line between rapid burning and explosion was recognized. Properly used, powder burns rather than explodes, and the rate of burning can be regulated by the size, and to some degree even by the shape, of the granules. Black powder appeared in various compositions for different uses and the particles were glazed.

Flintlock owners had often used two powders, one for ignition in the pan and another for the main charge. A very fine powder worked well in the pan and a much coarser powder served for the heavy charge, being relatively slow burning. When only one powder was used it was a compromise. Even in the twentieth century there were "duplex" charges in self-contained ammunition, and some tar-

47

get shooters used the new smokeless and black powder together. From 1800 to 1850 black powder continued to be the universal propellant, becoming more and more controlled in performance.

America's Civil War had enormous influence on sporting weapons, for the lure of government sales drove firearms inventors and would-be inventors into frenzies of activity. There was little standardization by either North or South, the smoothbore musket and the repeating rifle appearing in the same battles. There was the long-range sniper and massed infantry, there was political bias influencing armament good and bad, and there were hard-headed generals with outdated ideas. In one of the most vicious bloodlettings of modern times there was also a grisly lesson about firearms: there would be no more muzzleloading wars.

When the holocaust at Gettysburg had ended, methodical recovery of abandoned battlefield weapons revealed mute evidence of the common soldier's terrible fear. A large percentage of the muskets picked up had been loaded repeatedly, one charge atop another. A total of 37,574 such muskets were checked. Some 24,000 were loaded. About six thousand had a single charge; some 12,000 had two loads each, and 5,999 had more than three loads. One barrel contained twenty-three loads.

Once a musket is improperly charged the unloading process can be time-consuming. Without a "worm" on his ramrod to grasp the offending load, the soldier or hunter is helpless, and even completely equipped the trooper is probably incapable of such an operation while under attack.

So the touted "simplicity" of the musket was not always helpful.

Conical bullets rather than round had been used for some time but the Minié bullet, perfected by Captain Minié of the French army, was revolutionary. It had a hollow base, was undersized for the bore, and could be rammed home easily in a rifled barrel without the force previously needed. Upon discharge, the base cavity expanded and filled the rifling. It could have been a great boon to sportsmen, but it was brushed aside by modern breechloaders. The rifled musket of the Civil War had many of the qualifications of the Plains rifle and with a caliber of .58 could be deadly for one thousand yards. Such ranges were impractical for hunting, but it had sufficient accuracy for battle use to six hundred yards.

Although American gunsmiths are credited (especially by Americans) with practical development of several firing systems, it was usually Europeans who took the key first steps. The pinfire, a very practical gun using an enclosed cartridge, was invented by a Parisian gunmaker, Casimer Lefaucheux. It amounted to a cartridge containing both powder and bullet (or shot) with its own integral firing pin. Breechloaded, it was fired by the hammer striking the pin, which discharged a primer on the interior of the cartridge. The French inventor patented his design for a fowling piece in 1836 and the gun was a break action, the breeches notched at the top to receive the pins.

The cartridge was rolled paper with a metal head, looking remarkably like modern shotgun shells. When displayed in London at the Great Ex-

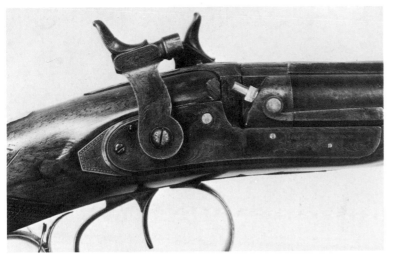

Sam Colt, Daniel Wesson (opposite, left to right). Joseph Manton percussion shotgun (left). Jennings rifle, (below, from top) North repeater, North with sliding lock, first Sharps, 1850–51, second Sharps model. Early revolving repeaters (lower left) are Wheeler above Jennings. Colt cylinder carbine over Colt Paterson rifle (lower right).

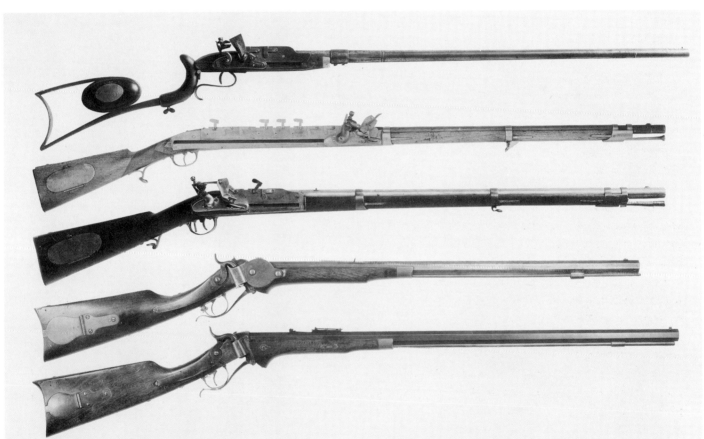

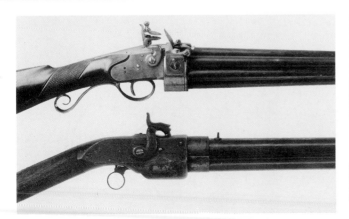

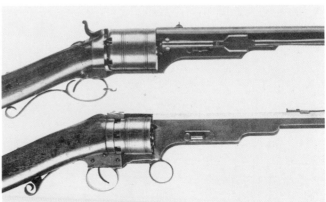

Wood pigeon (right) is favorite game of European gunners. French 12-gauge pinfire (below) rests on powder flask. German caplock is ornate 24-gauge. Dreyse needle gun (opposite) was forerunner of modern bolt action. Needle-like firing pin pierced cartridge and detonated primer at front of case. Model shown is Prussian military rifle.

hibition of 1851, the pinfire was introduced to the world—and to criticism by firearms experts suspicious of newfangled gimmickry. Joseph Lang, a London gunmaker, recognized the new system as progress. W. Greener deprecated it, possibly in part because it was a French innovation. British guns began to appear in pinfire and some were still in use well into the twentieth century.

Pinfire rifles, pistols, and shotguns gave good service but they could not fire the heavier charges usable in solid breeches. Through the development of cartridge arms the main difficulty has not been so much the actual firing device as the problem of containing it. It was difficult to make an opening breech that could withstand high pressures as well as a solid breech. Thus the muzzleloader could outperform all comers in measured tests.

A strong breech that opens easily is simple in general description; in practice it requires the exact fitting of large pieces of metal, and the var-

ious latchings, although never as dramatic as new "systems," have been worked out only with ingenuity and knowledge of metallurgy. Fitting a breech can be more complex than installation of the most delicate decorative inlays.

No one can say who invented the integral primer that works with self-contained ammunition, for there were so many types of limited success that only the skilled student can even follow them. However, the really strong bolt-action breech got its start with Nikolaus von Dreyse of Germany, who worked for Johannes Samuel Pauly of Switzerland. The shop was in Paris and their association lasted from 1809 to 1814.

Pauly had a patent for a centerfire, breechloading system using a self-contained cartridge with a primitive primer as early as 1812. If his invention had been widely accepted, the later percussion cap might have been skipped entirely, but he was truly ahead of his time. Napoleon Bonaparte

*Opposite (left to right),
Mississippi rifle, model
of 1841, model of 1855
with Maynard tape primer,
Colt infantry musket with
revolving cylinder, and Sharps
single-shot cavalry carbine.
Old postcard (below) shows
hunter's fashion of early
days in California.*

said so when he turned down the invention for army use. Pauly failed in the promotion part of his business and turned to other things.

Dreyse continued to work along Pauly's course and came up with a bullet which contained a primer in its base, similar to the later American Volcanic. When breechloaders weren't accepted he built a muzzleloader with primer fired by a long firing pin, or "needle." The term confused the firearms picture, for any rifle containing a long firing pin was likely to be called a "needle gun" in the years that followed. By 1836 Dreyse had a true bolt-action needle gun which changed the course of European warfare. It was the Dreyse bolt-action rifle that fought a series of wars and the type appeared on both sides in the Franco-Prussian conflict of 1870. It was a long time before bolt action was accepted in America. Only a few strays appeared on the plains and in the mountains.

Breechloading and repeaters advanced almost simultaneously, developing rapidly during the middle of the nineteenth century. Three makes of repeaters were prominent in the Civil War: the Spencer (said to be Abraham Lincoln's favorite and one with which he shot a target), the Colt revolving rifle, and the early Sharps. The Spencer carried its magazine in the stock and worked with a simple lever action. Later experts considered it the best rifle of its time, but lighter Winchesters appealed to the western trade particularly, and the Spencer plant closed its doors.

By 1865 it appeared that the muzzleloader's time had run out, though there still were

many in use thirty years later, especially shotguns. The military choice then and for some time later was largely singleshot breechloaders which fired heavy bullets attractive to big-game hunters.

Shops where the first pioneers' guns were made could hardly be called factories. Until the Civil War there were seldom any model numbers and there was little standardization, even in the matter of caliber. The Hawken rifles, although they had common characteristics, retained individuality, and so did guns of other early makers. Today's design need not be exactly like last week's if there was no assembly line and few standard parts. During and after the war, the bigger gun concerns got their start. For the first time there was demand for quantity production of particular models.

Names that were to be famous in the firearms field later on moved through a series of enterprises, partnerships, and companies along with other names soon forgotten. Leading manufacturers of today can trace their companies' lineage back for nearly one hundred and fifty years, but the beginnings often involved builders who became famous separately under their own names. One such company is Winchester, whose name has been so long associated with firearms that it has been applied loosely to all repeating rifles at one time or another. Modern literature and showmanship make it hard to believe there was any other kind of rifle at one time, even as Colt was used to mean any and all revolvers in the West. There was no such monopoly, making for a sort of pseudo-authoritative simplification.

Some rifles which were built for only

short periods, like the Spencer, may appear to have led down blind alleys of design, but some of their features were used in guns that became basic. The Winchester repeaters are generally traced from the inception of the Hunt repeating rifle of 1849. Walter Hunt's hollow-based bullet with its integral powder charge was a long step toward a practical repeater. Lewis Jennings, a machinist, made improvements in the design, resulting in a new patent while he was working for George A. Arrowsmith of New York to whom Hunt had assigned his original patents. Then came Courtlandt C. Palmer of Connecticut, a financier who bought the patents and made arrangements for manufacture of five thousand Jennings rifles by a Vermont firm.

Up to this point none of the names is familiar to any except dedicated firearms historians and collectors, but now appeared one that stayed: Benjamin Tyler Henry, master machinist born in New Hampshire in 1821. He was shop foreman at Robbins & Lawrence, who were to make the Jennings rifles, and the H that appears on the base of current Winchester rimfire ammunition stands for him. Then came Horace Smith and Daniel B. Wesson. Smith improved a patent assigned to the manufacturers. Both he and Wesson were gunsmiths.

The rate of the rifle's fire had been speeded up to twelve shots a minute and tallow-filled grooves on the exterior of the bullets had been installed to reduce leading. But the venture was not a financial success and Palmer, the backer, allowed production to stop in 1852.

So names that were one day to be world famous in the firearms field disappeared for a time while disappointed men undoubtedly tinkered with improvements, sure a breechloading repeater could succeed. It finally surfaced as a pistol under the name of Smith & Wesson in 1854, employing the general principles of the Hunt rifle with a magazine below the barrel. Henry worked for Smith & Wesson, and Palmer was the backer. Smith & Wesson lasted only a short while that time and became the Volcanic Repeating Arms Company in 1855. The incorporators still were Palmer, Smith, and Wesson but some of the stock was owned by a man named Oliver F. Winchester, a clothing manufacturer in New Haven, Connecticut.

So some of the most famous names remained together and a geographical center of the firearms industry was established. The repeating-rifle business wasn't profitable and Winchester saved the company by taking over a large part of the property to cover his loans to it. There were knotty problems of design in a business that tended to move in many directions toward mechanisms so far unheard-of. The Volcanic Repeating Arms Company became the New Haven Arms Company. When B. Tyler Henry made design improvements the organization became the Henry Repeating Arms Company, and then in 1867, the Winchester Repeating Arms Company. There are volumes of such maneuvers in the history of most firearms with old names, and sometimes the colorful name with its historical connotations is retained when all semblance of the original firm disappears.

Its time was getting closer, but the repeating rifle suffered from its earliest ills. The newer rifles were still in smaller calibers than hunters of heavy game wanted and the ever-present difficulty of breech strength haunted designers.

The Volcanic rifles at first had the powder charge contained within the hollow-bullet base, though there was not enough room for a heavy powder charge. Henry, shop superintendent, headed a redesigning move which altered the gun so it could fire rimfire metallic cartridges. It was covered by an 1860 patent. There was a two-flanged firing pin which struck on opposite sides of the rim, and the rifle was .44 caliber. That was to be a very important cartridge size for several reasons.

The Henry had a tubular magazine under the barrel and was loaded from the front. The tube was open on the bottom for most of its length and thus vulnerable to dirt as well as to being easily bent. The 1866 Winchester rifle and carbine appeared in almost the same silhouette as more than a hundred years of later Winchesters. A loading port was placed in the right side of the receiver, making it possible to enclose the magazine, the cartridges being pushed in from the rear. A spring closure for the loading port came quickly and a wooden fore end appeared. The Model 1866 Winchester was both a musket and a sporting arm. It handled .44 cartridges with either rounded or flat noses and had a brass frame.

The 44 Winchester Center Fire, or .44-40, was minimal for big game but it had the advantage of being readily adaptable to pistols as well as rifles, so that the frontier hunter carried only one

57

kind of ammunition. It was widely used in the Model 1873 Winchester. That rifle was built for fifty years as a centerfire arm and for much of that time as a .22 caliber rimfire. It was the Model 73 from which the first famous "One In One Thousand" rifles were chosen. Some of them were ornate; others were quite plain, being premium-priced because their barrels were judged especially accurate.

When the Winchester rifle got its final name it had already come far in development, and others associated with it had disappeared along the way. Winchester, the clothing manufacturer, gave it his name just as it began the successful part of its long career. The case of the Sharps rifle ("Old Reliable" in later days) was exactly the opposite: when Christian Sharps disappeared from the scene the rifle that continued under his name had barely begun its evolution. He invented the Sharps falling-block action and received a patent on it in 1848 when working in Cincinnati. He had previous experience in the government armory at Harpers Ferry, Virginia. The Sharps, slayer of thousands of bison, began as a percussion rifle using paper cartridges.

The early percussion Sharps, like the later cartridge models, operated with a finger lever under the breech. In loading, the operator pushed the lever downward, lowering the breechblock. He inserted the paper cartridge and when he closed the breech the sharp edge of the rising block sheared off the end of the paper container. The gun was fired with a nipple and percussion cap, as were muzzle-loaders, but Sharps devised automatic feeds for the caps. In military use some of the rifles used the May-

nard tape-primer system, a row of primer pods located on a tape, much as with later cap pistols. There were problems with automatic primer feeds and historians are sure that many hunters preferred to place the cap by hand.

Sharps left the firearms business around 1866 and only his name remained for later developments. A series of partnerships and companies disappeared so by default the rifles were made by the Sharps Rifle Company about 1874. Eventually built in Bridgeport, Connecticut, the Sharps was then marked "Old Reliable."

The action was strong and bulky and the rifle achieved its fame by throwing heavy bullets with great accuracy from large powder charges. When metal cartridges took over there was little change in Old Reliable's outward appearance. Clinging to the old design brought some problems, notably with a firing pin that had to be driven from the side and with a rather flimsy extractor, but it was the best known of the "big" rifles of buffalo days.

If its modest beginnings can be termed a "gun company," the Remington name has headed firearms manufacture longer than any other firm. In the beginning it was less romantically tied to great guns than were the names of Winchester and Sharps, but it had become a production firm early in the game while other soon-to-be famous builders were entangled in the agonies of design and financing.

The best known of the Remingtons was Eliphalet, who put together his first gun about 1816, near Ithaca, New York. Actually, his lesser-known father had been a gunmaker. The Remingtons began

Old postcard (opposite) showed the abundance of game in the Yellowstone Park region. Winchester '73 rifle, "One In One Thousand," with wagon wheel was special grade (below) with octagon barrel and checkered wood. Model 1866 Winchester (below) with Oliver Winchester's portrait and volcanic rifle and pistol in background.

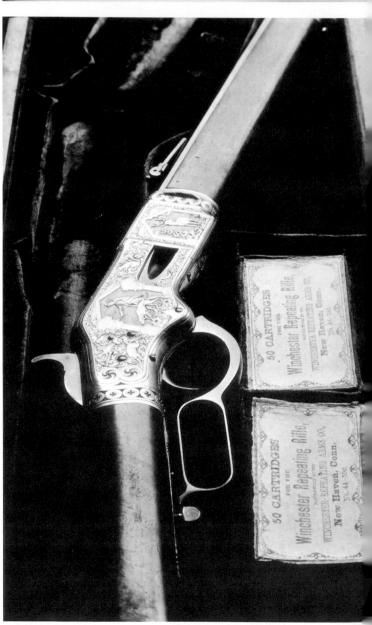

not with pinfire or percussion, but with flintlock, and they were making precision target barrels long before the other present-day companies had been named. It is said that some 200,000 Remington arms were supplied to Union forces during the Civil War.

Since they were more manufacturers than original designers at first, there are other names on most of the more colorful firearms advances. A man named Leonard M. Geiger designed a rolling breech during the closing years of the Civil War and Philo Remington, son of Remington's founder, bought the patent rights and hired the inventor. It became the Remington rolling block, and although it did not see war service it was declared the finest rifle in the world at the French International Exposition of 1867. The rolling block was to go forth with the Sharps and others to "win the West" with throaty booms alongside the crackling repeaters.

Since both were bigbore game rifles, it is natural to compare the Sharps and Remington as contemporaries. Most critics consider the rolling block more advanced and more durable but it could not match the fame of the Sharps. In the words of firearms historian Leighton Baker, "Shooters are notoriously conservative and after all those years of big side hammers they were slow to take to a hammer in the middle of the action."

The shooters had accuracy together with great bullet weight; they had rapid fire, even if in different packages, and they were ready to enter a golden age of shooting. At no time has marksmanship and its tools been so greatly respected and romanticized.

60

As the transition from muzzle to breech-loading began, changes in American game habits had not yet started in the West. In the East, deer hunting was becoming more difficult because of increased hunting pressure but the whitetail had not changed its basic habits. Squirrels were still there. Elk and buffalo were gone, and some feathered game disappeared from metropolitan areas. The ruffed grouse, ever a resident of civilization's borders and cutover timberlands, may have been more plentiful than ever. There is no way of telling. The moose still held forth in the Northeast. There was more hunting for sport than there had been during colonization.

On the trails west there were plenty of buffalo, seemingly an inexhaustible supply, and although the bison were an important commodity they had not yet been commercialized. Lack of transportation was one reason, but railroads were abuilding.

The elk was something of a plains animal, at least part of the time, and could be hunted somewhat as the buffalo was hunted, although it was much more intelligent. Like the mountain sheep the elk became more and more of a mountain and timber resident as settlers arrived. The historical pattern was that the elk spent summer in the hills and winter on lower ground, where there was less snow. When pressed by hunters the wapiti "moved back" and abbreviated its seasonal migrations. The plains rifle was good for elk and buffalo, as well as the mule deer which lived in both forest and plains along with the grizzly. The pronghorn (more of a goat but called an "antelope") was always a lover of open spaces.

While antelope never had much commercial value, they were important as a source of meat for pioneers. Later they were to be considered game for long-range, flat-shooting rifles but for a long time they could be killed with almost any rifle—or even smoothbore muskets. Their natural curiosity and witless dependence on their own whistling speed made them careless and easy marks for patient stalking. There was the business of "flagging," in which a hunter could conceal himself and then wave a rag or hat until curious pronghorns came to investigate. If the animals had not been recently hunted they could be coaxed to within shotgun range, and the time and care expended on the kill was not important to someone with a hungry family. The pronghorn had changed its habitat somewhat, naturalists believe, going from the grasslands to sagebrush in a natural evolution, as the buffalo, and later range cattle, used the grass and allowed sagebrush to spread. Originally, sage had been found only on higher ground.

Prairie birds, especially the great sage grouse, prairie chicken, and sharptail grouse were staples of diet for lonely travelers of the West. They were easily bagged with smoothbore muskets and the occasional true fowling piece. Their plenitude would last until plows had broken the seas of native grasses and the market gunners had come to the Midwest. On the Pacific Coast, the valley quail was too small to be paid much attention at first. Market gunners had already taken their share of eastern game but as the ringing steel hammers carried the rails westward, the time of the buffalo and prairie chicken was coming.

3

Sharpshooters and Showoffs

xamine the bison. When the Spaniards called them "Indian cattle" they were not far wrong, for although the buffalo was not domesticated it was ever available for the Indian's food and shelter. Before the great slaughter there were more bison than people in America. As a game animal the bison was a failure because it lacked cunning, was addicted to slavish herd behavior, and was plainly visible in most of its habitat. The poorly documented "woods buffalo" and the "mountain buffalo" disappeared early.

To the student of firearms the buffalo is important because it was the object of the world's greatest sustained hunt, a hunt that involved millions of animals and thousands of hunters over a period of years. From it developed the buffalo gun and the marksmen who used it. This hunt was a test for hundreds of makeshift guns that did not really make the grade.

The Indians used the buffalo for meat, its hide for clothing and shelter, and its chips for fuel. The white man traded for the robes and ate the meat as he traveled the frontier. As the robe trade ended, hide hunting began. Hide for leather was more valuable than pelts for robes. When the herds disappeared professional wolf hunters killed and skinned their prey. Finally, the buffalo bones that littered the Plains were gathered for buttons, chemicals, and fertilizer. The horse Indians of the Plains were subdued when the buffalo were decimated.

The time of the buffalo gun was only about fourteen years, between 1870 and 1884. About 1870 German tanning processes first made hide hunting profitable and by 1884 the herds were gone. At one time the American West supported an estimated 75 million animals.

Until hide hunting began, the buffalo population was healthy enough, and it may be that the early robe hunters and meat seekers actually prevented overcrowding and destruction of the habitat. As it was, much of the Plains was overgrazed. Before they had guns the Indians drove buffalo to a bellowing, tangled death over "buffalo jumps," which still can be viewed in the West. With horses they rode alongside to kill the bison with lances, arrows, and short-barreled trade muskets. The white men used revolvers at close range from horseback and anything else that would fire a ball, whether adequate or not. Some of this hunting was for sport, with European nobility participating in these lavish slaughters.

When the leather business began, the real shooters appeared with their booming single-shots and shooting sticks, their creaking wagons and professional skinners, and their hundreds of pounds of ammunition. All that went before had been relatively inefficient.

Some years before the hide hunting started in earnest, meat and robe shooters like William Cody learned the principles of stand shooting, a matter of chopping down animals from concealment rather than chasing them with horses. This took a heavy-caliber gun and careful riflery, while the crazy pattern of buffalo running might be executed with almost any sort of maneuverable weapon. In buffalo running, if one shot did not stop the animal, more could be used, and light repeaters and pistols would work at arm's length. If the animal did not go down immediately there was little concern.

But the stand shooter was not mounted and did not want to show himself. He based his success on killing his game within a small area and upon the instantaneous stopping of any animal that started to move away from the slaughter zone. He needed an accurate and powerful combination. In that day of black powder, velocity was supplanted by bullet weight, and such things as "hydraulic shock" were unheard of. The big bullet had to have penetration for certain kills and it had to be able to smash any bones in its path. At a later day, when the velocity of lighter missiles produced their own killing efficiency, the old buffalo guns and their ilk were called "punkin rollers."

At first there seem to have been a great many .50-caliber, breechloading Springfields, called "Long Toms," probably Civil War leftovers. There were some muzzleloaders, as well as some Henry and Winchester repeaters. Best known was the Sharps breechloader with its enormous side hammer and heavy action; and the Remington rolling block killed its share. Since the stand shooter did little walking the rifle might weigh as much as sixteen pounds.

Frank Mayer, one of the best known of the hide hunters, used Sharps rifles, switching from a 40/90 to a 45/120/550. That designates .45 caliber, 120 grains of powder, and a 550-grain bullet. Virtually all of today's rifle bullets travel faster than the estimated fourteen hundred feet per second of the Mayer load, but the bullet weight was about the same as that of current elephant cartridges and the striking power about half as great. Mayer used twenty-power telescopic sights from Germany.

Rifle development had gone in two directions, toward firepower and light weight in the repeaters, toward long-range accuracy and big bullets in the singleshots. The lever-repeater's comparatively springy action would not handle the mighty loads used by most professional buffalo men.

Most of the shooting was done around midday, leaving daylight time for the dirty work of skinning. The shooter, usually the head of the party, located a band of animals and approached them from downwind, keeping to cover. A herd of thousands consisted of several small contingents, otherwise grass would not be available to all. One professional said a bunch of a hundred was about right.

There is disagreement as to the ideal range. Some shooters tried to get within a hundred yards, but were generally satisfied with two hundred. Others reported that three hundred yards was an ideal distance. If they got too close they ran a danger of stampeding their targets with smoke and noise. Many of them preferred to shoot with a forked branch or with folding "shooting sticks" in the form of an X.

There, with his ammunition spread out beside him and with a spare rifle to use while the other cooled, the professional could adjust his breathing, contemplate the wind and weather, and plan his shoot. He studied the animals before him and by their feeding pattern he tried to choose a leader, a cow that was to be his first victim, and

65

*Christian Sharps' (top)
breechloader became the
most popular single-shot of
the Civil War and Western
expansion despite some design
shortcomings. Buffalo hunting
could become dangerous for a
man on foot as shown in
C.M. Russell's work of
about 1892 (below).*

when his big, blackened front sight steadied behind her shoulder he might deliberately shoot a little too far back for a quick kill. A humped-up and slowly dying cow, smelling of her fresh blood, could hold the other buffalos' attention and they might even butt and shove her. Then the big rifle boomed swiftly and regularly, and the day's tally grew.

If one animal seemed about to bolt and lead others away it had to be stopped instantly, which required a single perfect shot. The hot rifle was exchanged for the ready spare, and the marksman used water for cooling the barrels.

A long way from the railhead, with his wagons and skinners awaiting his signal from a distance, the hunter might hear other rifles on other stands and he often identified them from their reports. He was in the red man's land and he took the red man's food, so he had eyes for all that happened on the miles of swaying grass under a cloud-racked sky. He saw the waiting vultures and the gray wolf's shadow below the ridge, and far beyond his selected targets he was ever watchful for unusual movement by other buffalo.

The average was much less, but there are stories of shooters killing more than a hundred bison from a single stand. Their efficiency was based on dropping the animals close together for the skinning crews. Mayer sought a kill of fifty animals a day. A hunter named Brick Bond is said to have averaged ninety-seven buffalo per day in the fall and winter of 1875–76.

When the shooting was finished the wagons were pulled up and the skinning began, often with the assistance of horses in pulling off the hides. The big flattened bullets that had done their job and gone almost through the animal were likely to be found immediately under the tough and stretchy skin on the other side. They could be melted and cast into new bullets, and fired again.

The buffalo killers had their reputations among the Indians, some of whom realized that the buffalo gun meant the end of Plains life as they had known it. There are many stories of surrounded buffalo hunters who took a dreadful toll of hostiles at long range, and the big rifles took part in numerous battles alongside other guns. It was twenty-eight buffalo hunters who stood off six hundred warriors in the battle of Adobe Walls (June 27, 1874) in the Texas Panhandle. Concealed in two stores and a saloon built of sod, they fired for two days.

Hostile Plains Indians of any tribe studied prospective white victims with care and from a distance, and special attention was paid to anything that looked like a buffalo hunter or a buffalo gun. Indians could mount wild charges and circling attacks, and braves learned to fire under a racing horse's neck at close range, but the horse Indian afoot was at a dangerous disadvantage and even at long range the buffalo gun was a horse killer.

The enormous herds were broken into many smaller units most of the time and their migrations were ill-defined by hunters. They moved in order to find new grass and only in loose formations could individuals graze satisfactorily. Their numbers were deceptive, and although a railway could be blocked while passengers fired gleefully from win-

dows there might be no bison at all a few miles away. In some cases there were special railway excursions to accommodate "hunters" who left the cars only to cut tongues or pieces of succulent hump.

Some of the biggest kills of the hide-hunting days were made in the Midwest, and Kansas and Nebraska were favored hunting grounds. After the Santa Fe Railway reached Dodge City in 1872, it became the "buffalo capital of the world." There was a large kill in Texas and the final slaughter petered out in the Northwest, with a few bands surviving in foothills of the Rockies. It was all over by 1884.

Reports of easy money in buffalo hides attracted a motley collection of "hunters," some carrying guns unsuited to the task. Many of them had outworn their welcomes where they had come from and as newcomers to the West they often had no notion of how to survive on the plains. They starved, froze, and were sometimes scalped.

For most of the nineteenth century all American game was for sale. Most big game was harvested too far from centers of population to appear constantly in city meat markets, but upland game, shore birds, and waterfowl were staple items. Problems of refrigeration caused diners of the time to accept game that would undoubtedly be discarded as overripe by today's standards.

On the ever-restless grass oceans of the Midwestern prairies, gunners and their dogs marched like skirmishers, and the prairie grouse rose ahead of them, individually or in great flocks, rolling like a cloud that continually lowered in the distance as the birds alighted again. As the day wore on, birds were flushed for the second or third time and marksmen who were shooting for a living did so with little waste motion. They filled the wagons that followed them, a part of the logistics of a business that resembled a military operation.

Since much shooting was done in warm weather, spoilage was accepted as a calculated risk

and some of the birds never reached market. Except when killed at the outskirts of cities, the bag had to be hurried to a railroad and shipped with primitive refrigeration—wooden barrels and a minimum of ice.

The prairie chicken, or pinnated grouse, faded rapidly with the breaking of prairie sod and the onslaught of efficient gunners, although to some extent it adapted to cropland. The sharptail grouse of the Northwest was able to adapt better because it spent more time in brushy ravines and strands of trees, and thus survived when most of the prairie chicken's home had been converted to agriculture. It was not found in the areas of concentrated market gunning.

Plover and curlew, generally taken in larger quantities in spring, were considered delicacies. Adam Bogardus, an Illinois commercial hunter and one of the best of his day, says: "The best places for shooting golden plover and curlew in the earlier part of their stay with us are the burnt ground of the prairies, where the grass is beginning to quicken, and those close-eaten and bare spots in the pastures." That was in the Midwest. His preferred tactics included a buggy with a fast horse, and he recommended driving rapidly, as if intending to pass a large flock on the ground, then stopping suddenly to fire.

The same procedure was recommended for an athletic gunner on foot. When plover were trading between fields on their restless days, the shooter could operate from a stand, probably lying on the ground. Since speed was important in any event, Bogardus preferred a breechloader for all such shooting. In fact, he had been quicker to accept the breechloader than many of the well-known shooters of his time.

For most market gunners it was a strange mixture of business and pleasure. They went to great effort and endured considerable hardship eking out a precarious living, but in their scant records there is almost invariably running comment on the sporting aspects of shooting.

On occasions, when most of the game had spoiled before it reached the market, the economic loss was almost recompensed by the fine shooting that preceded it. And while most of the gunners killed birds sitting on water or land, they prided themselves on their ability as wing shooters and carefully noted scores made when "shooting flying."

The ruffed-grouse hunters of the East had a special place in market gunning, partly because grouse hunting was even then so unpredictable that hardly anyone could make a living at it, although the bird was regarded as the supreme culinary treat. Frank Woolner, New England grouse historian who interviewed some of the old hunters in their later years, found that most of the hunters considered grouse shooting a sort of vacation with expenses paid, and they went back to other occupations when the shooting season was over.

While prairie shooters measured their bag by barrels and wagonloads, twenty-five ruffed grouse killed in a day were an occasion. In partridge cover there were no resting flocks to be bagged on the ground. The birds had to be collected one by one. While Bogardus says most of the grouse were killed from trees, shooters of 1900 proved to later sportsmen that they could more than hold their own in wingshooting, and it is likely that their woodcraft and grouse knowledge will never be surpassed.

It is doubtful whether commercial hunting had any great affect on grouse populations. The eastern hills had already been settled and abandoned in many instances, the tiny family farms with their apple orchards and stone fences being absorbed by the persistent forest. While the land went back to its past there were periods of new growth—wild grapes on the settling stone fences and birches to crowd the aging orchards. Such scenes were ideal for ruffed grouse who budded the apple trees and drummed at the edges of the lumberman's clearings.

Like the breed of hunters that used them, the strains of dogs that sought partridge in 1880 are largely gone, their descendants purposely changed through crossings with dogs of other inclinations. Those early workers, largely setters, were slow-moving, cautious hunters able to "hold" the skittish ruffed grouse while pointing from a considerable distance. There were Gordon, Irish, and English setters, most of the pointers of the day being farther to the south or west. The grouse dogs might wear home-stitched boots as the long season advanced, their pads suffering from weeks of contact with rocks and thorns.

Farther west, Bogardus said his favorite dogs were crosses between pointers and setters. Dog breeders of today, striving for specialty performers, can only guess as to the contributions—or detrac-

WILD FOWL SHOOTING.

tions—of crossbreeding of a century ago.

In Woolner's investigations of the grouse hunters' equipment, he found that hunters preferred smaller shot than is used today. He reports that Clayt Adams of Oakham, Massachusetts, one of the best of the old-timers, used five and one-half drams of powder with one and one-half ounces of Number 11 or 12 shot in his 10 gauge. Until the arrival of the repeater, most of the grouse men used double guns, often cut short and without choke, and even with the muzzles belled (perhaps more of a mental than a physical aid, since modern studies indicate that belling a muzzle makes little difference). The grouse is a quick and close target. When the repeaters appeared, most commercial hunters preferred them.

In the case of the ruffed grouse, laws prohibiting their sale may actually have done more harm than good. They were never shipped in the quantities of waterfowl or prairie game, and when legal sale was finally stopped the price went up immediately and market hunting continued. Small numbers of these expensive birds could be bootlegged with little chance of detection.

The sinkbox gunner of the eastern seaboard saw dawn from a coffinlike box, neither boat nor raft, and lay flat on his back, his eyes barely above the level of hinged "outriders," or aprons, that kept waves from breaking over him. He was propped against a headboard and the muzzles of his long-barreled shotgun rested on the end of the box near his feet. It was nearly always a long-barreled gun. A short one was likely to fall back into the enclosure

and might discharge. Thirty-two-inch barrels were common and the gun was probably an 8 bore, although some 10-gauge guns were used.

His view was confined to a narrow expanse of sky and water and his field of fire was limited, but he had a huge raft of decoys properly located, and the broadbills or canvasbacks would appear in the proper sector when they set their wings and came in, their momentum fading as the broad muzzles swung up, coolly pointed to take their toll, probably one shot as the birds settled and another as they fought gravity for flying speed.

The coffinlike box of the battery became a real coffin on days when storms were sudden and the attending pickup boat was unable to rescue the tempest-tossed gunner. The effectiveness of his method was based on the fact that the box lay flat against the surface and from a short distance appeared to merge into the great raft of decoys. There was no defense against swamping except discarding ballast or manipulating the anchor to gain an inch or two of freeboard.

Dangerous though the battery was, in the years before it was declared illegal it was the most efficient means of killing coastal waterfowl. Market gunning for ducks was a going business for a long while, and more than five hundred commercial hunters operated on North Carolina's Currituck Sound alone.

There were commercial waterfowlers all along the eastern seaboard but Chesapeake and Currituck Sound appear most frequently in contemporary accounts. Not only did they have what appeared to be an unending supply of ducks, especially divers, but they were near enough to large centers of population for the kill to be kept fresh with ice until it reached the market. The 1880s were both a high point in the number of hunters and a beginning of the steady deterioration of waterfowl supplies.

There were other methods than the battery. Sculling boats, "brushed in" with foliage to appear as a drifting mass of flotsam, could be worked almost to the midst of birds on calm days. The sculler lay flat, alone or with another shooter. And there was good pass shooting from shore on hundreds of points and beaches, especially when the northers brought heavy clouds and sleety winds that kept the endless flocks moving and flying near the water. The eastern guns were mostly double-barreled in the heyday of market shooting, before the repeater. In the Midwest there were more singleshots, especially in muzzleloading days.

In the Midwest the mallard took the place of the canvasback and along the wide, slow rivers and their attendant marshes the working gunners used flat-bottomed boats that could be rowed across shallows and skidded on runners when the water froze.

Among market hunters there the breechloaders came slowly. There was the tedious task of reloading ammunition. The early paper cartridges could not withstand dampness, and once a shooter had his cartridges loaded he could not adjust his charges to changing conditions as the expert muzzleloading hunter did. During lulls in the shooting the man who used a muzzleloader could fill small tubes with complete charges and then ram them home quickly when business was good.

After the breechloader took over from percussion guns there was a period when those who did a great deal of hunting nearly always loaded their own ammunition. After 1900, factory cartridges predominated and the large ammunition companies discouraged sale of components for homemade ammunition. It was the great popularity of clay-target shooting after 1950 that brought back handloading, and with it came newly efficient tools and cases that could withstand multiple reloadings. Whereupon the large manufacturers began to advertise components.

Frontiersmen were the shooting heroes, not because their guns were best or because they were always the best shots, but because their livelihood, and sometimes their lives, depended on their guns. Their shooting contests always had been informal, the results hard to measure in terms of rifle precision or muscular control. They shot at live turkeys staked out at long distances from their firing line, and at shorter distances they shot at turkeys' heads and a variety of "marks." If these matches came close to the conditions of actual hunting, they told little of the ultimate in precision of man or gun.

While the great buffalo slaughter was building to its climax and professional shotgunners made great inroads on feathered game, the best long-range target shooters were developed not in prairie hunting camps but in Britain and on the European mainland.

"Long range" is a relative term. The buffalo standers fired from two hundred to three

The Creedmoor rolling-block was a special model produced by Remington for the United States match with Ireland. It and the Sharps Creedmoor had precisely adjustable tang sights and special stock wood. Buffalo hunters usually used less refined models but actions were the same.

hundred yards. Five hundred yards or more was impractical for them. Since their big bullets described a sharply curved trajectory, they could not hit at those extreme distances without knowing the range. No matter how accurate the gun or steady the hold, misjudgment of a few yards could produce a miss, and waving grass carried no yardage markers.

So it was primarily the military riflemen who took interest in shooting half a mile or more, and it was the Europeans who led the field, for after the Civil War, American military units turned to polish and parades and for a time did hardly any shooting at all. The British were the long-range leaders and they standardized their competitions through their own rifle association, which was established in 1859. Like the American Rifle Association, organized in 1871, it was loosely associated with the military and some of its activities were subsidized.

From 1860 on, the English had a one thousand-yard range at Wimbledon. Their first formal long-range shooting was done with their 1853 Enfield, a muzzleloading rifle much like the 1855 Springfield that many Americans carried in the Civil War. With proper sighting equipment it could be counted on at such ranges. In the meantime, Americans considered six hundred yards the maximum for practical shooting and, in a strange about-face from tradition, the British Volunteers could easily have outshot the gleaming New York National Guardsmen.

In 1862, while American riflemen were fighting their bloody war, the Scots challenged the British Volunteers to a long-range match at eight hundred, nine hundred, and one thousand yards. It became an annual affair. The Elcho Shield, produced by the English as a trophy for annual champions of the British Isles, was the prize. Since Ireland was engaged in recurrent rebellions against the Crown at the time, no Irish team was invited. They were allowed to compete finally in 1865 and in 1873 they won the championship and looked for new worlds to conquer. They immediately challenged the United States.

America had a new National Rifle Association and a new Creedmoor range on Long Island, patterned after Britain's Wimbledon. The Irish

had addressed their challenge to the Amateur Rifle Club, evidently not knowing America now had a national association. The challenge was accepted, the ruffled feelings of the National Rifle Association smoothed, and American tryouts began. The Americans had a long way to go. In their earlier matches the Canadians and British had outscored them badly.

The British by that time had some really fine target rifles with fine sights. It was a stipulation of the match that the Americans must use American rifles, although some of the best U.S. marksmen had used British Rigbys and Metfords in the past. When the challenge was issued, Americans simply didn't have the guns to compete.

Remington and Sharps jumped into the breach, drawing from the models that were booming on the prairies a thousand miles away—the buffalo Sharps and the big Remington rolling block. They used special wood, vernier tang sights, and globe front sights with spirit levels. With the manufacturers' patriotic honor in jeopardy they even put up the $500 ''good faith stake'' required of the Americans.

The cartridge was the 44-90, but the commercial loads of 300- and 370-grain bullets were supplanted by a 500-grain bullet of hardened lead, capable of bucking wind better at one thousand yards. The tried and proven muzzleloading British Rigby was .45 caliber and had been the top match

performer for almost a decade. In a way it was to be competition between the breechloader and the muzzleloader, the former still unaccepted for precision target shooting.

More than a century later, when newspaper sports sections are filled with news of the most esoteric games and athletes, it is difficult to imagine the impact of the Irish invasion. Despite long, dusty roads to the scene, there were eight thousand spectators at Creedmoor, held back by ropes.

For the most part, the Irish were better at the longer ranges. The Americans won at the shorter ones. And although it may have been a fluke win, the Americans did triumph. One Irishman fired a bullseye on the wrong target, enough to make a decisive scoring difference. On the other hand, one American shooter had a defective cartridge that could not reach the butts.

Muzzleloader and breechloader finished in a virtual dead heat and one leading American competitor loaded only his case and powder from the breech, loading his bullets from the muzzle. Similar systems were still in use many years later by top target shooters.

Prone positions varied greatly. Some competitors lay on their backs or sides and held the barrels with their feet or legs, while others used facedown positions as did later experts. Whether the steadiest position might well have developed from side or back will never be known, for those were poor military positions and military form was almost universally accepted soon afterward.

Nattily dressed Irish competitors made the Americans appear drab. The match was observed by nobility and was a social event of international significance. Its importance was so great that newspapers posted almost shot-by-shot telegraphic reports in both America and Britain. It was the beginning of serious international shooting, although for some time that meant English-speaking teams only.

The Germans were engaged in building and firing their fine precision target arms. The Prussians and the French fought a war using the Dreyse "needle gun," a true bolt action, and others very similar.

A long way west of Creedmoor a man named Wright Mooar was living a busy life with a pair of Sharps rifles. He had killed a great many buffalo and would kill more than twenty thousand with the two rifles before he was through. It is doubtful if he had ever heard of Creedmoor.

Since the competitions were not well standardized there was no way of actually choosing a world's champion shotgunner in the days of market gunning. Perhaps the most persistent claimant was Adam Bogardus, who wrote discerningly of his methods. He was a large and powerful man and much of his shooting was to demonstrate endurance as well as accuracy.

He began his competitive gunning in 1868, when he was already long experienced in the field. He was a winner at trapped pigeons, glass balls, and other aerial targets for thirty years after that. In New York City in 1879 he tried to break 5,000 glass balls in five hundred minutes. He missed 156 of them; but beat the time limitation, taking only a

BUFFALO BILL'S WILD WEST
AND CONGRESS OF ROUGH RIDERS OF THE WORLD.

BUFFALO BILL SHOOTING ON HORSEBACK AT FULL SPEED.

SHOOTING GLASS BALLS

TO PALACE

HUNTING BUFFALO

little more than six hours for the demonstration.

Bogardus is important to sporting arms for several reasons. His career spanned the entire gamut from flintlock musket (with which he began shooting as a youth in New York State) to hammerless double, the repeater, and smokeless powder, and he was articulate in his textbook on shotgunnery, *Field, Cover and Trap Shooting.* If he was not modest in his personal claims, that was in keeping with the style of professional gunners. He retired from active competition about 1890, although he did considerable shooting after that.

Dr. W. F. Carver, a close friend of Bogardus, was of the same caliber but a "world championship" meeting between them was hard to arrange because cautious backers felt they were too evenly matched. They did shoot numerous exhibitions together.

In shotgunnery the transition from muzzleloader to breechloader was well under way by 1870. The essentials were present, including self-contained shells and satisfactory extraction, and in 1874 Bogardus publicly acknowledged the breechloader as superior. Even then, however, the muzzleloader was called on for extremely heavy charges by waterfowl gunners.

Bogardus, like many shooters of the day, favored heavy shotguns. His first high-grade gun was an English Greener muzzleloader (the British had an early start with quality guns for American sportsmen), but it weighed only seven and one-half pounds and Bogardus felt that was much too light. His recommendation for a shotgun for all-around use was 10 gauge with thirty-two-inch barrels and weighing ten pounds. He conceded that something lighter might be satisfactory for grouse hunting. At that time, of course, some waterfowl guns were as large as 4 gauge and weighed twenty pounds. In 1883 Bogardus was using a W. & C. Scott & Sons.

He handled ten-pound guns easily. However, his complaint that the seven-and-one-half-pound gun was a hard kicker might have had something to do with the measurements of his favorites. He chose a "drop" of about three inches, a very crooked stock by modern standards and likely to transmit heavy recoil. At that time there was a tendency toward crooked stocks, possibly an American carryover from the upright style used with the old Kentucky rifles.

In the matter of recoil, the very large gauge of many nineteenth-century guns was not always a measure of their shot charges. A study of their actual loadings reveals that a 10 gauge of that time was likely to carry no more shot than a 12 gauge of later date. A good 8-gauge load included no more than 1½ ounces of shot, while the modern three-inch, 12-gauge magnum is regularly loaded with 1⅞ ounces. And waterfowl shooters who used the largest-bore guns could have them built heavy, since little walking was involved.

Both Carver and Bogardus appeared with Buffalo Bill and in other shows. Another shooter of the same caliber, although of a less flamboyant nature, was Fred Kimble of Illinois. He numbered among his attainments the violin, figure skating, championship checkers, and invention. He is credited with the development—though not the invention—of shotgun choking. His skill enabled him to take advantage of an extremely tight pattern that lesser shooters could not use. He made his personal discovery of choke boring in 1867, although various gun authorities had promised dire consequences for anyone who attempted to squeeze the speeding shot through a reduced muzzle.

Kimble, modestly stating he was no gunsmith, bored a choked barrel for a muzzleloading musket, tested it, and found the pattern unsatisfactory. Rather than take out the breech plug again to work from the stock end, he simply started to bore out the constriction from the muzzle. When he thought he had reached a cylinder bore he tested the gun again, found an extremely tight pattern, and learned he had accidentally left in just the right amount of choke. He then had a gunsmith named Tonks build him a 9-gauge singleshot muzzleloader with choke, the gun with which he was to practice the waterfowling wizardry that made him famous.

At first, even the great Kimble simply could not take advantage of the extremely close-shooting gun, but practice produced a deadly long-range combination. He claimed for his gun a range "thirty yards more than that of any other shotgun in Illinois."

Kimble sought no patent. Patent applications are a bit vague on the subject, but W. E. Greener of England, who made no claim to inventing the choke, was its persistent proponent and developer. The British continued to lead in shotgunning techniques.

Major Charles Askins, an arms expert of later years, pointed out that the extreme killing efficiency of Kimble's gun came from some features not available to more modern shooters. Shot deformation is the factor that destroys modern shotgun patterns, and it was at a minimum in a large-bored muzzleloader. There is no forcing cone to pinch the shot together as it starts down the barrel and no cartridge case to impede its progress, and the large barrel causes a minimum of shot crowding.

Kimble easily won duck shooting contests with the gun and once fired a tie in a pigeon-shooting match with Bogardus. A proposed contest with Carver never materialized. Carver was something of a prima donna, ready with alibis if something went wrong, blaming guns, powder, and manufacturers, as though his ability were in doubt—which it never was. In exhibitions, he seemed to outshoot Bogardus most of the time, though Bogardus was still considered tops.

In 1869, when unemployed, twenty-three-year-old Bill Cody crawled from the shade of a wagon to meet Ned Buntline at Fort McPherson, Nebraska, the greatest promotion of guns and shooting the world has ever known was about to begin. It was the starting point for the professional exhibition shooter who was destined to be a public hero for the next fifty years.

Buntline, whose real name was E. Z. C. Judson, was a writer of colorful western prose: fact, fiction, and a mixture of the two. He interviewed Cody about some Indian fights and saw in him the ideal subject for western yarns. Cody had a back-

84

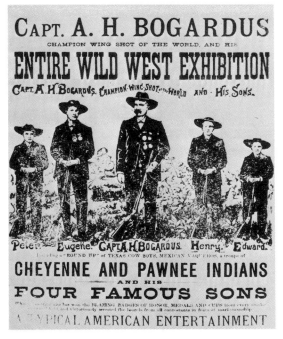

ground as freighter, professional buffalo hunter for
railroad construction crews, and army scout, and he
had been in Indian combat. As a showman he made
the most of his striking looks, with his goatee and
flowing hair; he even wore white buckskin suits with
thigh-length riding boots. Even in advanced years
he cut a dashing figure. Cody accepted the glitter
and exaggerated publicity of show business but he
was not a charlatan. He was an exceptional shot and
an exceptional horseman, and his flair for showmanship was luck for him and for Buntline.

It was reported that in a buffalo-run-
ning contest against Billy Comstock, a famous U.S.
Army meat hunter, Cody not only killed more buffalo than his opponent but then defeated him thir-
teen to nine while riding without saddle or bridle.
He used a .50-caliber breechloading Springfield.
Some historians believe the story is a product of Ned

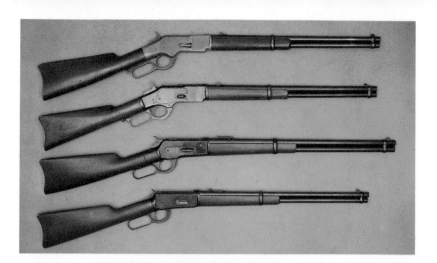

Winchester (left, top to bottom) Models 1866, 1873, 1886, 1894. The 1894, designed by John Browning, is still a popular deer rifle. Dr. Wm. F. Carver (below) attempts to shoot 60,000 wooden balls thrown in air in six days. A scene at New Haven, Conn. shows busy thrower, important to a demonstration. Aerial ball and block shooting continued for many years as test of guns and shooters.

Buntline's busy imagination.

Will Cody was thoroughly a showman, even when he was making a precarious living as a buffalo hunter, for the .50-caliber Springfield rifle he used was named Lucretia Borgia and his buffalo horse was named Brigham. After he became Buffalo Bill he served as a hunting guide for the famous, including the Grand Duke Alexis of Russia, and then went East to become a professional performer.

But Buffalo Bill's contribution to sporting firearms was not so much his own shooting performances as the fact that through his Wild West Show he brought to prominence some of the greatest shooters of the time. Because of that vehicle and others patterned after it many obscure names became well known, and their dramatic demonstrations of accuracy and endurance were instrumental in the development of firearms. The exhibition shooter may have appeared at a time of "entertainment innocence," but the names of Buffalo Bill and members of his troupe are known today by thousands who cannot name a trapshooting champion of the past fifty years.

There were better shots than Phoebe Mozee, according to her contemporaries, but not much better. Her later name was Annie Oakley, she was born in 1860 in Ohio and started shooting game for the table while very young. There were six other children in the family. In her teens she was a market hunter and at twenty-four she surfaced in an exhibition of endurance shooting. She challenged a .22-rifle record of 984 X 1000 targets set by a Dr. A. H. Ruth of New York, and although she did not break

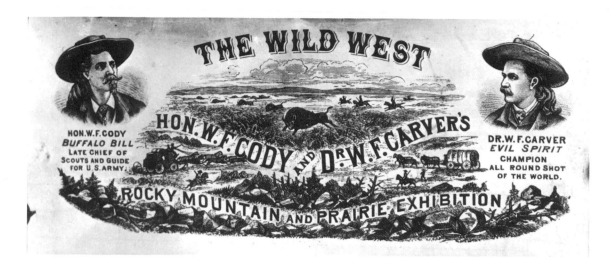

the record she was instantly prominent in the shooting game. Shortly afterward, she and her husband, exhibition shooter Frank Butler, were hired by Buffalo Bill for his show.

It was said that Butler could outshoot her. If so, it was academic. What attracted audiences was her slight frame. Through the years shotgun champions tended to be solidly built specimens, and a slender woman was something new in the jarring business of long-run shooting. Annie won a great number of live-pigeon and clay-target matches against top men shooters, and while her achievements as an exhibition shooter may not be measurable, some of her trapshooting was. In 1922, at sixty-two, long after her exhibition days were over, she broke one hundred straight sixteen-yard clay targets. She was a headliner for years and when Buffalo Bill's entourage went abroad she was a favorite of royalty.

Here was no wide-shouldered giant like Bogardus, who swung ten-pound shotguns so easily. What gun did she use? Her first high-grade gun was a 16-gauge Parker, an American entry against the respected English doubles. The first Parker shotguns had gone on sale in 1868. Charles Lancaster, the English gunmaker, built her a seven-and-one-half-pound 20 gauge and later a pair that weighed only six pounds fourteen ounces each. Buffalo Bill presented her with a Sauer.

Ernie Lind, the famous exhibition shot of a later day, says in his book on trick and fancy shooting that Annie used six double-barreled shotguns in 1894. They were two Lancasters and two Scotts from Britain, a Belgian Francotte, and an American Parker. In addition to repeating rifles, she had Lancaster and Holland double rifles. Her usual shotgun charge was an ounce of shot.

Perhaps the most advertised and colorful shooting of the Buffalo Bill show, and Cody's specialty, was from horseback at close-range aerial targets with "rifles." At first they really were rifles, but when embarrassing—and dangerous—holes began to appear in the walls and windows of arenas, the shooters shifted to shot cartridges fired in smooth-bored Winchester Model 73 .44-40 guns, the same as rifles in outward appearance. Some Marlin models and other Winchesters were used later on. The Model 73 load held 20 grains of black powder and one-fourth of an ounce of chilled shot. At that time shot sizes were not well standardized and the designations might be confusing to modern shooters.

The Buffalo Bill show faded early in the twentieth century and there was a gradual change in the status of the showman shooter. Annie Oakley taught marksmanship in her later years and like many other of the exhibition shooters appeared in vaudeville. Exhibition shooting lost its interest for the general public, and the later demonstrators generally appeared before audiences with a special commitment to firearms.

Bogardus, Carver, and others of their time undoubtedly received financial considerations from the manufacturers of their guns and ammunition. Carver, especially, was not above calling a competitive powder "dangerous." They were not directly employed by manufacturers, however. Many twentieth-century shooters have been directly employed by large firearms companies.

One pair of experts, Ad and Plinky Topperwein, bridged the transition period. Topperwein started his professional shooting career in 1889 in San Antonio, Texas, near where he was born. He shot in vaudeville, traveled with a circus, and in 1901 was hired by Winchester. He married Elizabeth Servaty, who was a Winchester factory employee and who became one of the most spectacular woman shooters ever to appear. Bearing the new nickname of "Plinky," Mrs. Topperwein set a world's trap record in 1904, and she went back to work for Winchester as a professional shooter along with her husband. Before her death in 1945 she made 193 runs of 100 straight at sixteen-yard trap and twice ran 200 straight.

"Topp" was interested in what might be called marathon shooting, and endurance was highly valued by the various "champions" from 1870 until World War I. Perhaps his performance on wooden blocks in San Antonio in 1906 is a record. He began firing at blocks thrown into the air by a corps of tossers, and using the remarkably efficient and lightweight Winchester Model 1903 semiautomatic .22 rifle he shot at 72,500 targets with only nine misses in a period of ten days. The Topperweins performed for U.S. military personnel of both world wars.

Any sort of marathon exhibition "record" is confusing for there are no hard and fast regulations for them. Topperwein's throwers used rules laid down by Doc Carver with targets no more than two and one-half inches in diameter and with the throwers standing at least twenty-five feet from the shooter. Much later, Tom Frye, who worked for Remington, used a Remington Nylon 66 .22-caliber autoloader and fired at 100,010 wooden cubes, missing only six. But in this case the throwers stood close to the shooter. Who can truly be called the "marathon champion" is a question not likely to be answered.

Modern exhibition shooters have displayed incredible skill with mass-produced American guns. Herb Parsons of Winchester could throw seven clay pigeons into the air simultaneously and break them all with a pumpgun. Perhaps undisputed champion of the pistol demonstrators was Ed McGivern, whose pudgy hands had little resemblance to the "talons" of the fictional gunfighter. Nevertheless, McGivern, who died in 1957, once fired five shots from a .38 Smith & Wesson revolver in two-fifths of a second, making a playing-card-sized group at 15 feet.

Late in the twentieth century the measured accuracy of all sorts of competitive shooters is greater than those of the good old days. Representatives of the ammunition companies occasionally give demonstrations but there is less enthusiasm for "spectaculars" of gun handling. In some phases of shooting there was for some time a unique classification. For example, "amateur" trapshooters competed for prize money. "Professional" shooters (those employed by firearms firms) competed in their own division without purses.

There are still shooters who have become legendary among other shooters, but the day of public fame is gone.

4

Big Bullets and Biggest Game

There has never been an ideal gun and load for all heavy game at all times, although with personal danger involved, making the best of many possible choices gains special importance. Those who first used guns against truly large animals found their choice less complicated than did later shooters. They had no option between heavy bullets and high velocity, and very little between hard and soft bullets. So, regardless of the structure of dangerous game, the hunter tended to choose the largest gun with the largest bullets he could fire quickly and with reasonable accuracy.

Although there are many game animals which can be dangerous occasionally, there are only a few which may attack hunters without provocation, and will regularly do so if wounded. There is the elephant, heaviest game of all, generally shot at close range. There is the African Cape buffalo, sullen, unpredictable, and hard to down. Its opposite number in Asia, the gaur, the world's largest bovine, weighs up to a ton and a half. And the rhinoceros, a tough carryover from another age, is dangerous through size, stupidity, and nearsightedness.

The great killer cats—lion, leopard, tiger, and jaguar—are deadly in their own way but swifter and more fragile, and thus pose completely different problems for the hunter.

In between are the great bears—polar and grizzly—and their relatives. They are classified as thin-skinned, yet are so heavy of bone and muscle that modern hunters often use calibers designed for Africa's behemoths.

The beginning of sport hunting with guns in Africa is a shadowy business, for none of the first elephant guns could possibly have been adequate and failure might have been fatal. Elephant hunting with guns began before Lewis and Clark faced the plains grizzly. Sport hunting, however, received little attention until somewhat later.

There have been three main reasons for hunting the world's most dangerous game. Commercially it has been a profitable business, especially with the elephant and its valuable ivory. Defensively, there has always been the danger of rogue individuals, especially deadly in areas where aboriginal residents are poorly equipped to protect themselves. And for sport the largest and toughest game has always been a challenge to people who either enjoy the danger of facing a possible killer or feel some necessity for proving their bravery to themselves or to the rest of the world. Some hunters have had all of these reasons at the same time.

The bravery required to confront dangerous game and the varying codes of conduct involved in it have been belabored in both fiction and nonfiction to the point where readers are inclined to be cynical about the matter. It is true that a modern sportsman equipped with the latest rifles and with an experienced armed guide or "white hunter" beside him has a tremendous advantage over any animal, but the element of danger exists. No matter how flippant the reportage by a modern arms writer, there is almost invariably some delving into the psychology of the situation, a thinly disguised question as to how the individual will perform under this kind

Before high velocity, bullet weight was only way of dealing with big game. British doubles (preceding pages) were of bores seldom seen later. Top is a Holland & Holland 8-bore hammer gun. The 4-bore Greener (below) shows distinctive side safety; the W. & C. Scott is a 4-bore. Such doubles were intended as close-range "stopping" guns, heavy but short.

of pressure. Stories by professional hunters are filled with cases of wealthy clients who wanted the name without playing the game and have considered the collection of trophies an unpleasant duty for the maintenance of status. Scoffers are inclined to term the entire process a throwback to savage ordeals for proving the bravery of the new warrior, with little respect for the fact that many otherwise civilized persons enjoy danger—or the illusion of danger.

Colonel Charles Askins, certainly one of the more adventurous modern hunters, with a lifetime of war, skirmishes as a border patrolman, and big-game hunting around the world, makes a personal statement of the matter in his book, *Asian Jungle—African Bush*. Askins, a prolific writer about guns and their use, first gained fame as a national pistol champion, but was named by a contemporary gun expert as "the best all-around shot with everything in the United States."

Says Askins: "It is good to sometimes be afraid. It sharpens the reflexes to run your head into the halter of mortal danger. To become afraid, for then, and not until then, can you be sure the courage is there to shoot your way out of the cul-de-sac which an over-exuberance of hunting passion has gotten you into."

Although not all hunters agree concerning the attractions of fear, there is no doubt Askins neatly expresses the feelings of the loose cult of hunters who seek dangerous game and often pay well for the privilege of meeting it.

The choice of guns for heavy game is complicated by the fact that the purpose is not only

to kill the animal, but also to prevent it from attacking before it dies, a very difficult proposition for a hunter armed with a singleshot weapon, however large its bore. Even when the huge old muzzleloaders appeared with two barrels the problem was far from solved. Gunmakers and big-game hunters continue to debate the nature of "shock" and are unable to explain why one shot kills a large animal instantly and a very similar hit on another day seems to have little immediate effect.

Colonel Robert L. Scott, Jr., when he wrote *Between the Elephant's Eyes*, reported a museum study he made of an elephant's head before a hunt actually began and said: "Only an engineering marvel of construction could be large enough to hold giant ears, mighty trunk and heavy tusks and yet be light enough for a head.

"In reality, within the head of no other animal must there be so great and efficient provision for the absorption of shock as in the elephant."

He then describes the "crenelated bone armor" which shields the elephant's brain, a bone wall sixteen to eighteen inches thick all about it. So not only is the elephant's brain almost surrounded, but that casing is so constructed as to be somewhat spongy, a texture very difficult for a bullet to penetrate and perfectly designed for shock absorption.

What shooters term "knockdown power" in the elephant's case becomes stunning power or "stopping power." Although small-caliber bullets properly placed are quite capable of killing huge animals, as many hunters have proved, they are less likely to "turn a charge." If an elephant is

struck hard enough in the skull it will be momentarily stunned and turned from a charge, even though the bullet does not penetrate to a vital organ.

Scott examined the elephant's skull, heard the recommendations of more experienced campaigners, and explained that the best location for the shooter was at one side of the game, where he had a ninety-degree profile. Then he was to aim at an imaginary point between the eye and the earhole, which is hidden by the ear flap. But such procedures, highly successful for the close work of early ivory hunters, were sometimes not possible to follow in emergency situations.

John Hunter, a professional guide of royalty and the famous for many years, tells of shooting a charging elephant through a point at the center of the skull three inches higher than a line from eye to eye, then finishing the animal with a shot through the neck with his 475 Jeffrey. In a discussion of rifle caliber, he says: "If you hit a rhino or buffalo in the correct spot you can kill him with a light-caliber bullet. But if you are stopping a charge you must have a bullet with sufficient force to knock the animal off his feet." Recent scholars of bullet-striking power explain that the blow would not knock the animal down but cause it to fall because it is stunned, a matter more of terminology than of meaning.

Hunter explained that the earlier African hunters dealt with game that was relatively tame and could be approached by shooters who could then pick their shots. Most famous of the smallbore shooters who used rifles ordinarily chosen for deer was W. D. M. "Karamojo" Bell, an ivory hunter who did

The Westley-Richards single-shot percussion gun (below), with "monkey tail" breech, was a powerful stopping rifle although later hunters of dangerous game preferred double guns, and even later took to the bolt. The double was king about the time of 1904 lion hunt (opposite). Early elephant hunters often operated in heavy cover at close range (opposite, below).

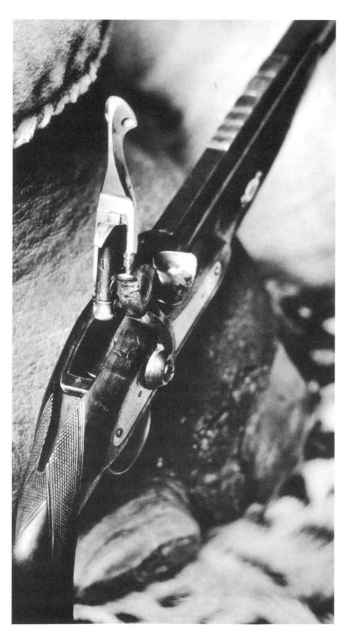

his shooting at close range. Much of his ivory was taken with a 7mm bullet. The Cape buffalo and India's gaur presented a problem similar to the elephant in that they have extremely heavy bone structure and their skulls are protected by bulky horns. Here, too, the problem is not so much the eventual death of the animal but the need for quick stopping.

The dim-eyed, truck-smashing rhinoceros, sometimes described as "armor-plated," has weight and power. African hunters credit it with less cunning than either buffalo or elephant, but it was a rhinoceros that finally killed famed Charles Cottar, the African guide who survived attacks by many other dangerous animals.

The agile, soft-skinned cats and bears presented other puzzles to the first big-game hunters. Later they were to be complex problems of bullet expansion coupled with bullet penetration. But to begin with, the only solution was as heavy a missile or missiles as men could launch.

The first elephant hunters evidently attempted it with smoothbores of 12 and 16 gauge. Then, around 1840, there were reports of really big muzzleloaders for the purpose, and even though the breechloader and self-contained ammunition were being perfected shortly afterward, the really heavy charges could be assembled only in muzzleloaders. Some smoothbores were as large as 4 gauge and the first ones available were singleshots. The urgent need for a follow-up caused double-barreled guns to appear shortly, and the feeling seemed to be that if so much weight were necessary anyway to dampen recoil, it might as well be applied in a second barrel.

Although singleshots (right) were popular, especially with British army officers who might have limited means, the ideal equipment was a matched pair of big-bores (opposite). Big Rodda 4-bores are fully rifled and very rare. The singleshot (below) is a highly respected .577 Snyder.

Many years later the double-barreled elephant gun was chosen for other reasons. The first guns were not very handy in operation and the howdah pistol could serve almost as well when British sportsmen operated from an elephant's back against India's tiger. The howdah pistols, whether single- or multiple-barreled, were arm's-length weapons and are depicted in use as a tiger leaped for the elephant's passengers. First made in flintlock, the caliber might be as large as .75. The fine British percussion pistols of a later date were of somewhat smaller bore.

Smoothbored elephant guns were used long after rifling had taken over other forms of shooting. In early days of elephant hunting the contact was at pointblank range and the smoothbore was easier to load, generally being overbored for the loose ball that could be rammed in quickly. Most of them were described by "gauge" rather than caliber. Gauge refers to the number of round balls of bore size required to make a pound. Thus, 4-gauge balls would weigh one quarter of a pound, or four ounces.

There were several efforts at solving the accuracy problems of shoulder guns in such giant sizes. A number of rifling systems were tried, some of which employed bullets cast with ribs to fit the grooves. "Oval boring" was a system of casting the barrels slightly out of round in such a way as to give the bullet a slow twist without grooves and lands, the twist increasing near the muzzle.

Near 1900 there was a move to muzzle rifling. That is, the greater part of the barrel was smoothbored but there would be a section of rifling near the muzzle. As the bullet neared the muzzle it

Two of the most dangerous of African game are the evil-tempered Cape buffalo (top), shown in typical cover, and the maned lion (bottom), one of the most desired trophies. Hunters of recent years have the same problems as those of the pioneers, despite modern optics, rapid transportation (right), and more efficient calibers.

would encounter increasingly deep lands and grooves. That system was patented by Colonel George Vincent Fosbery, inventor of the Webley-Fosbery automatic revolver. The best-known name for muzzle rifling was the "Paradox," the rifled section being only two or three inches long. After the patent expired, other British gunmakers used muzzle rifling under a variety of names.

The rifled muzzles were usable with shot and made good combination guns in some cases, but the largest bores were too heavy for most shotgun use. Nearly all the largebore guns came from Britain in the early years. German builders became increasingly active as smokeless powder arrived.

Cartridges for early elephant guns were a problem to designers because extraction of such long tubes was sometimes difficult, especially if the case was made of paper with the consequent tendency to swell with moisture. Even when the cartridge case was brass the extra length gave trouble. By 1900 there was already a variety of bullet constructions, bullets already capped with brass and sometimes lined with iron. Explosive shells were used to some extent.

Bullet weight was virtually the only desire at first, but when round balls began to give way to elongated ones there were some early efforts at making hollow bullets that would have the advantages of great sectional density (a relationship of weight to length) without becoming too heavy for shoulder guns. The early bigbores were very heavy, many of them around twenty pounds, one reason perhaps that gunbearers were a standard part of most

African or Asiatic hunts. Some sportsmen had several gunbearers, a sensible precaution against gun failure and a substitute for repeating rifles. The gunbearer remained on the scene with modern guns, partly because the later hunter usually wanted to take two or more calibers for a variety of game and partly to assure a ready back-up rifle.

None of the early big-game guns was intended for long-range use. "Long range" is a relative matter. The long shot of three hundred yards as sometimes used by a modern pronghorn hunter, or even a nineteenth-century buffalo man, was completely out of the question for the bush hunter of Africa or the explorer of Asia's jungle. A hundred yards was a long shot there if heavy game were involved and fifty was a more common distance. Ivory hunters often fired from much closer than that. Hence, bullet shape was relatively unimportant, the only reason for improved sectional density then being increased penetration.

There was no reason why a bullet weighing a quarter of a pound could not be accurate at long range, and many of them were. The problem was simply a matter of trajectory, an exaggeration of the buffalo gun's chief fault. If the gun was to be used at long range the distance had to be known, almost to the yard, and when the bigbore rifle became a double-barrel there was a special problem for long-range shooting, this one unsolvable, even with the finest of sighting equipment. The double rifle had to be "regulated."

"Regulating" is a highly complicated business which contributes greatly to the cost of double rifles and is a matter of constructing the gun so that both barrels shoot to the same point of impact. It still must be handled mainly by trial and error with involved machinery or the painstaking use of wedges between the barrels. Once both windage and elevation have been worked out for both barrels, the two can be guaranteed to shoot to the

same point at only one range, to be decided with considerable soul-searching by the builder.

Once the double gun is zeroed at that point, the user is also restricted to the same charge of powder and the same kind of bullet that was used in the sighting-in. Any experimental charges promise to change the zero and probably cause the two lines of fire to diverge. There have been, of course, ballistic freaks in which the two barrels have for some reason continued their compatibility to longer and shorter ranges, and sometimes even with changes in loads, but such things are beyond the control of any craftsman.

Applied to modern rifles, the calibers of the first "express" rifles would be large indeed, but when James Purdey introduced that name around 1856 a caliber of .500 was considered very small. The first express rifles were muzzleloaders and did extend the range somewhat with a belted ball, but their velocity of less than two thousand feet per second,

with a bullet of less than 500 grains, was not sufficient for the Asiatic gaur, Cape buffalo, rhino, or Asian or African elephants. There were hair-raising stories of failures. So most of those express rifles were relegated to the "medium" rather than the "heavy" class.

Breechloading, smokeless powder, and improved bullets changed caliber assessment. When the term "Nitro Express" came into big-gun gunnery it represented potent cartridges and had a connotation of power, which helps the sale of cartridges.

Shooting the largest game was for many years almost exclusively a European sport. When Americans did go to India or Africa they simply followed British customs, used British equipment, and wrote books about it. After the West's buffalo hunts were over, American guns leaned more toward rapidity of fire, convenience, and accuracy, and the manufacturers did not compete with Europeans in the construction of "stopping" rifles for a long while.

African elephants have been killed with smallbore rifles at very close range, but such work is only for experts in both guns and anatomy. Before hunting pressure increased, it was possible to stalk to the very center of a herd. Now the gunner usually fires from a longer range.

Around 1900 a hunt in Asia or Europe was enormously expensive and required a very long time by ship, rail, and boot. American sportsmen were barely aware of the close-range stalking of enormous beasts in the half-light of bush or jungle, or of the droves of plains game viewed by a safari procession. Theodore and Kermit Roosevelt brought Africa to them in accounts of a full-scale bloodletting; in 1909 they banged away at African game, were gone for nearly eleven months, and brought back nearly five thousand items for display at the Smithsonian Institution. They took some American rifles along, but when it came to the buffalo, rhino, and elephant they had Holland and Rigby .500 double express guns. Their American rifles were Winchester lever actions, especially the Model 95 with its powerful-appearing lever and box-magazine construction. That model was in .405 and .30-06. There were also a Model 94 in .30-30 and a Model 1886 in .45-70. From all accounts available, the Model 95s were used more than the other American rifles, serving well as "medium" arms. The then-popular .405 was commonly loaded with a 300-grain bullet, similar to the weights of current "medium" bullets, although driven at lower speed.

The Roosevelts, of course, had the world's best shooting advice and their expeditions left little to chance from the standpoint of organization. However, some of their shooting tactics would be viewed with distaste by modern sportsmen. In his book *African Game Trails*, the former president tells of what sounds like a strafing attack on a group of four Cape buffalo. He says: "The biggest of the

four stood a little out from the other three, and at him I fired, the bullet telling with a smack on the tough hide and going through the lungs. . . . Kermit put his first barrel into the second bull, and I my second barrel into one of the others, after which it became impossible to say which bullet struck which animal, as the firing became general."

Although such an attack would be frowned on by later hunters, it must be remembered that a big score was highly valued by Americans of the day and that some of the safari bags were enormous, overcrowding museums and trophy rooms.

But while the Roosevelts were doing Africa the big way, other Americans made shoestring invasions of the Dark Continent. The mists of time have obliterated the campfires of many unnamed adventurers, but Charles Cottar bears mention again because of his audacious approach to plain and bush with what many correct sportsmen would consider a minimal deer rifle. Later he was to become a famous African hunter and a guide. The Oklahoman had killed a number of Canadian grizzly bears with a Winchester Model 94 in 32 Special (ballistics closely akin to the ubiquitous .30-30) and evidently saw no reason why it would not work on the beasts of Africa. In 1912 he took it there.

Everything worked out well, although his first African trip was a series of close escapes. He killed lion, buffalo, hippo, and rhino with his coyote rifle and was so delighted with Africa that he packed up his family and moved there, becoming famous for shooting motion pictures of African game, sometimes during provoked charges. At that time Cottar's

Ornate Merkel double rifle (below) is one of the finest of continental "heavies". Merkels such as the fine over-under and side-by-side shotguns show deep stock carving typical of Germanic guns. Over-under (right, top) is a lightweight 12-gauge sidelock of 1956. The boxlock double (right, bottom) was made in 1936.

"light" rifle was a 250-3000 Savage Model 99 lever action and his "heavy" was a 405 Winchester. Between the two he killed all of the dangerous game.

"Karamojo" Bell's methods of working his way into the very center of an elephant herd and then killing his game with a 7mm or other smallbore would be even more dangerous today. Wilder animals will not permit such careful shooting. Apparently his later years were filled with hairbreadth escapes and, of course, his rifles were not truly adequate except when used at very close range with meticulous aim at vital organs, generally the brain. His cartridges produced about half the muzzle energy of acceptable modern elephant cartridges and used much lighter bullets. Users of such cartridges cred-

ited them with good penetration, but none could call them charge stoppers.

The double rifle was never popular in America and until bolt-action arms were accepted American hunters simply used European guns for heavy African game. When really powerful bolt-actions began to be used there was a great deal of comparing by various hunters on both sides of the Atlantic. Generally speaking, Europeans preferred doubles while Americans chose bolt action, but there were big-bored bolt actions in Europe from the beginnings of the Mauser system, the forerunner of modern designs.

The later arguments for double rifles were quite different from those urging their adop-

tion. It was now said that the user of a double had two complete rifles and that if one failed to operate he was still able to fire the second. Rugged simplicity of construction was at a premium and guns with exterior hammers were used well into the twentieth century. Double triggers have been widely favored on hammerless guns for the sake of simplicity.

Double users argued truthfully that they had two shots available instantly without the manual operation of an action under duress. The double was more quickly reloaded than the bolt action and some shooters learned to fire with spare cartridges ready in their fingers. And despite its weight of ten pounds or so, the double-barreled rifle was very fast to handle, simply because of its overall shortness and its

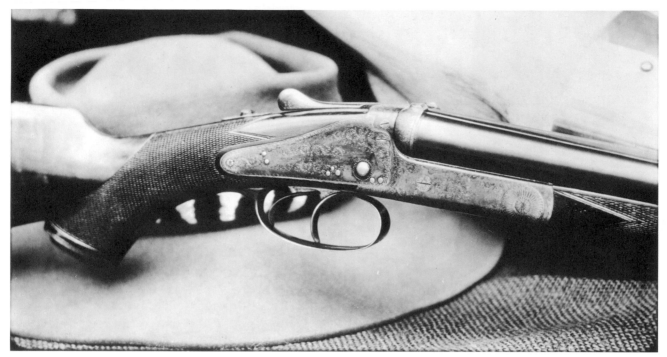

balance of weight between the shooter's hands. It was generally stocked much like a shotgun for fast use and pointed naturally at pointblank range.

Standard aiming equipment for the modern double rifle was leaf sights, generally wide and shallow, with different leaves for different ranges. There was no effort to get front and rear sights far apart because they could work faster when reasonably close together, still with sufficient accuracy. Telescopic sights and peep sights never were favored with the big doubles. Even though some scopes and mounts were built to withstand the lashing recoil, there were other things that could happen to them. Rifles for heavy game frequently received hard knocks. Then, too, use of peep sights or scopes somewhat restrict the shooter's view, a problem in dangerously close quarters.

Of the arguments usually forwarded for the double, that of its being "two complete rifles" was not quite true, as it was possible to jam the action so that neither barrel was usable. The speed of handling and natural pointing were accepted by all. Most common arguments against the double rifle were its great cost, the matter of "regulating," the restriction to close range, and the presence of only two cartridges without reloading. The bolt-action builders won most of the market in the end, but they had their difficulties.

Bolt-action rifles were relatively inexpensive and quickly recognized for their accuracy. They were not as short and easily handled as the doubles, and they required manual manipulation for a second shot but provided four or more cartridges for instant use. They were capable of handling heavy loads that lever actions could not, and they were ruggedly simple. Once emptied they were a bit slow to reload.

It was difficult to keep the heavy recoil from destroying the stock until extra heavy lugs were forged, and a magazine rifle tended to batter its loaded cartridges with recoil. Soft or fragile bullets might be so badly deformed they would not feed at all. When some of the first heavy-duty cartridges recoiled in actions heretofore employed for milder loads, the floorplate sometimes popped open, strewing essential ammunition on the ground while an elephant or buffalo was deciding to charge. Sportsmen who had not given their rifles thorough trials beforehand found themselves in serious trouble—but this was because the custom bolt actions had not been through the long testing of double barrels.

Bolt guns used their own cartridges because the double was generally built for a rimmed or "flanged" case, whereas most bolt systems employed rimless cartridges with a groove around the head to accept the extractor. Soon there was near-

One of the most desired of all heavy-game rifles is the British Holland & Holland with fine engraving (opposite) for .500 caliber and nitro powder. The Holland is now difficult and expensive to acquire. The red hartbebeest (left) was a prized tropy. America's most famous African hunter, Teddy Roosevelt, killed all of the heavy animals, sometimes with minimum armament.

duplicate performance in the rimless cases. Two cartridges, one British and the other an American adaptation from the English, really made the bolt action an African and Asian standby. One was the 375 Holland and Holland, the other the Winchester 458 African.

The 375 Holland and Holland Magnum is widely accepted as the world's all-around cartridge for big game. Although a bit heavier than necessary for deer and considered by some to be on the light side for elephant, it serves in both extremes. It is a fairly good "plains" cartridge and can be loaded with the heaviest solids, which make a good stopping cartridge. It is the top choice as the medium rifle for Africa, and ammunition for it has been available in the far places of the world.

The .375 began in England in 1912 as a flanged cartridge for double rifles and with a belted rimless case for magazine models. The bullet weights have varied but tend to be in the 270- to 300 grain category. Holland and Holland used a Mauser bolt action, and the American custom gunmakers, Griffin & Howe, began building rifles for the cartridge around 1926. The Western Cartridge Company was offering cartridges in 1925. Winchester produced a rifle for it in 1957 and other manufacturers followed suit. The Enfield action was widely used after World War II. Since muzzle velocity with 300-grain bullets is more than twenty-five hundred feet per second, the cartridge is good at moderately long range and a .375 rifle is a good candidate for scope mounting.

An excellent choice for Alaska's great brown bear and the white polar bear, the .375 has often been supplied with a detachable side scope mount

so that iron sights can be used when desired. Some feel that it alone can satisfactorily cover all big game if appropriate bullets are used for various sizes of animals.

The truly heavy rifle, the 458 Winchester, may well be the number-one cartridge in the world today. Not that its ballistics are greatly different from those of some English and German cartridges, but it has been accepted by Americans, who largely replaced the Europeans as Asiatic and African hunters. Introduced with a rifle for it in 1956, the .458 appears about to do for the "stopping" rifle what the .375 did for the medium rifle. Certainly a standardization of calibers has been needed, for there are many expensive rifles in far places where their owners can find no ammunition for them.

The 458 Winchester finds a nearly opposite number in England in the 416 Rigby, for which Rigby built rifles on a magnum Mauser action. There are similar German cartridges.

The most powerful commercially produced rifle and cartridge combination today is the 460 Weatherby Magnum, displacing the British 600 Nitro Express, introduced in 1903. The Weatherby cartridge was introduced in 1958. There are some who feel such speed for so heavy a bullet is not necessary. Jacques P. Lott, writing in *The American Rifleman* for February, 1972, says: "I find its 2,700 f.p.s. [feet per second] velocity well beyond that required for optimum performance on dangerous game, which I should place at around 2,300 f.p.s."

Bolt-action rifles for the heaviest cartridges have simple but important qualifications. Extraction, which deals with a large case, must be positive and many experienced hunters are meticulous in the polishing and sometimes relieving of the magazine feed area. A bolt which can bind when pushed or pulled at a slight angle is a hazard. Cartridges of extreme length are not favored because an excessively long bolt throw could be dangerous for an excited shooter who might not complete the operation and close the action on an unloaded chamber. Stocks are generally of dense and plain wood which must survive considerable battering, beauty giving way to utility. The sling swivel is usually located out of the hand's way on the barrel rather than on the fore end.

Modern hunters listing an "African battery" tend toward three rifles. The light rifle is generally used for deer-sized game at considerable range. Typical choices are the .30-06, .270, or one of the 7mm, equipped with scope sight. This rifle is not intended for use against the heavy animals.

In the medium rifle there has been disagreement between the proponents of high velocity and those of bullet weight. The .375 has long been the leader in this category, but in a number of African tours Roy Weatherby (see p. 129) and his friends made a strong case for a smaller bore and greater bullet speed. They proved that the 300 Weatherby Magnum could kill all species of African game. Its ballistics have been duplicated or near-duplicated by numerous "wildcat" cartridges. The 300 Winchester, which came somewhat after Weatherby's round, is very similar in performance and appearance and the 308 Norma Magnum, originated in Sweden, has similar ballistics.

Displayed (below) are all of the glories of the African big-game safari. The five guns are all large-bore rifles for heavy game, aptly leaning on a zebra-skin trophy. In the background is the typical safari-hunter's tent with open sides.

Before much of Africa's sports hunting was halted by political changes, there had been stringent regulations against the use of smallbore rifles on dangerous game. Although proponents of high velocity complained that such regulations were based on the concepts of blackpowder days, the rule-makers felt it was a way of curbing crackpot experimentation—and wounded game can be dangerous for weeks or longer. Many of the rogue animals responsible for unprovoked attacks are found to be suffering from old wounds caused by inadequate guns or native spears.

Although heavy bullets in the 500-grain class remained the favorites for the heaviest animals, the really big bores faded from use on thin-skinned animals such as cats and bears. In America, a great number of grizzlies have been killed with .30-caliber rifles, probably more with the .30-06 than any other, and the brown bear, a much larger relative, has also been hunted with these relatively small bores and some considerably lighter. Some brown bear hunters, however, have gone to the medium bores such as the .375 and the newer 338 Winchester. Asia's tigers have been killed from platforms with almost all sorts of guns, including shotguns with buckshot, but the medium calibers are usually recommended.

Smallest of the deadly game animals are the leopard of Africa and Asia and the jaguar of Central and South America, targets that present their own special problems for hunters.

The leopard is man-sized, probably never weighing more than two hundred pounds, but it holds special credentials as an ambusher when

112

wounded. Man-eating leopards, although rare, have been harder to find and destroy than tigers or lions, and one man-eater of Asia was blamed for 125 human deaths. The most common method of hunting is with a bait and with the hunters in a nearby blind. Hunting ethics accept baits for cat hunting, although often rejecting them for bear.

With such lighter-framed animals, bullet choice is much more important than caliber choice. Many dramatic tales of Africa have centered around the necessity for tracking wounded leopards in the bush, a business about which ethics of sportsmanship hover erratically. In addition to the disgrace of allowing a wounded animal to suffer there is the probability that the leopard will kill a person who had no part in its injury. So wounded leopards are followed, often with shotguns.

The assumption is that the animal will be confronted at very close range where buckshot will be an ideal defense. Ernest Hemingway, in relating one such incident, felt not even buckshot was necessary. He told of looking for a wounded leopard in thick cover with a pump shotgun, and since he did not trust the available buckshot loads, fearing they might jam the action, he preferred some reliable cartridges loaded with birdshot. Since even a cylinder-bored shotgun will fire most of its charge into a single hole at ten to fifteen feet, Hemingway apparently felt there was little need for buckshot. He inferred his choice of the shotgun was mainly for its speed of operation and natural pointing.

The jaguar, very similar in appearance to the leopard, has many of its characteristics but has not been hunted so widely—and since it lives in even thicker cover and farther from civilization, it has made fewer attacks on people. It is found south of the United States and north of Argentina.

Efficient shooting of dangerous animals requires not only some knowledge of anatomy, but an ability to assess a bullet's route from a distance. Despite countless diagrams, the elephant's brain may be hard to locate with certainty from an unfamiliar angle. The careful marksman may be able to aim a shot that will not only pass through a bear's lungs or heart for a sure kill, but will break a shoulder and immobilize it instantly. Such combination shots require not only good shooting and a knowledge of the game's anatomy but proper bullets for the job—and a bullet that will be extremely destructive in muscle might blow up against bone.

Charging animals become special problems and charging lions in tall grass can be virtually invisible much of the way. The charging buffalo, his brain shielded by tremendous horn bosses, goes with his head up and must be shot through the nose if the brain is to be reached. The shoulder is a more obvious target. Since the elephant also charges with his head up, the brain would be reached by shooting "somewhere between the tusks." So the killing of dangerous game can be complex and terrifying.

The bolt action has become the most popular rifle for dangerous game. It is a simple and reliable mechanism, born in the military and now a tradition in itself. Collectors pay great sums for the best double rifles, which may have had their day but remain jewels of craftsmanship.

5

High Velocity

Although firearms and ammunition have constantly attracted inventors and although some of the cleverest devices of history have been associated with guns, actual acceptance of new ideas by shooters has been slow. When self-contained cartridges took over from percussion guns, some manufacturers continued to use the high side hammers that had been necessary for cap and ball and for flintlocks before that. The Sharps rifle of frontier fame looked much the same, even after it was changed from percussion to centerfire. The big hammer had been there so long the shooting public evidently preferred to see it, despite the rather awkward firing-pin arrangement it made necessary. At any rate its silhouette remained after more modern designs appeared.

And shotgunners were so skeptical of the sleek appearance of the modern hammerless that some guns were actually made with dummy hammers to retain a traditional image. When damascus barrels were abandoned for much stronger material, manufacturers went to great lengths to color the new and better steel so that it would look like traditional damascus.

It is no surprise that extremely high-velocity cartridges were available before the public really accepted them. For that matter, the advancement from black powder to smokeless powder was gradual, and smokeless powder in its many forms was the key to high velocity, which was to mean lighter ammunition, longer practical range, and controlled bullet performance.

Smokeless powder, invented by an Austrian, Frederich Volkmann, was ready for practical use in rifles by around 1870. He made his powder with finely cut alder wood, and since the rate of burning could be regulated, the basics of high velocity were established. The Austrian government closed Volkmann's business on the grounds that it interfered with a government monopoly and after 1890 smokeless powder finally began to be accepted through the efforts of a number of chemists and ballisticians.

One of the very first big-game cartridges designed for smokeless powder has been in continual service ever since. It is the workhorse .30-30 Winchester for the Model 1894 rifle, the lever-action that has continued in use for nearly a century with only minor changes.

It started with a 165-grain bullet, still a good choice for deer-sized game, and the velocity was a little less than 2,000 feet per second, a long way from the magic 3,000 feet sought a little later. But outdoorsmen could not measure velocity and would not have known its meaning if they could. The rifle fired fast and flat for its time and its caliber; "thirty-thirty" sounded good in the same way that "Big Fifty" had sounded good when applied to the buffalo Sharps.

A list of other cartridges of almost duplicate ballistics appeared a little later, many having their proponents for real or imagined reasons, but the thirty-thirty (pronounced a little differently in various parts of the country, though generally coming out "thutty-thutty") has outlived a hundred more powerful and flatter-shooting cartridges. Almost a century after the first Model 1894 Winchester was produced in .30-30, a modern rancher owning a rack of custom rifles in exotic calibers will still carry a 94 as his saddle gun. Especially in the carbine version it is light and so flat it is hardly noticed under a horseman's leg. It became a standard in the Western Hemisphere from the Arctic through much of Latin America, and its popularity, especially in .30-30 caliber, made ammunition available in isolated communities. The number of rifles chambered for the cartridge is uncounted.

Lever-action thirty-thirties, especially of Winchester and Marlin make, have bounced in buckboards and wagons and later in pickup trucks, often poorly cared for and gathering a patina of rust, oil, and dirt. Sometimes they became so much a part of the horseman's gear that they hung with the saddle in the barn.

The 32 Special, almost a duplicate as to performance, was never so popular as the thirty-thirty. Charles Cottar confidently took his 32 Special to Africa.

Although westerners of the 1970s had largely replaced the thirty-thirties with more powerful rifles in their pickup racks, it retained its popularity in the eastern deer forests. In the back country it tended to hold respect. Jack O'Connor, former dean of American gun writers, quoted the Indian who terminated a discussion of ballistics and bullet "drop" by stating that such problems did not assail the thirty-thirty, which just went straight regardless of distance.

Smokeless powder was to eliminate much of the cleaning drudgery that went with black powder and it was to make for easier hitting at long and unknown ranges. Most of all it was controllable to an extent that black powder had never been. It is true that black powder had been made in various sizes of granules but its essential nature remained one of fast ignition, however mild its reaction.

Just a few students of the subject understood the difference between "explosion" and "controlled ignition," although the shooting public remained largely ignorant of it. The principle is simple enough, however complex the factors of control. When powder is ignited it expands in the form of gas that pushes the missile out through the barrel. If the expansion is gradual, a great deal of powder can be used and the projectile can be going at terrific speed by the time it reaches the muzzle, whereas powder that burns too fast will burst the gun. But the "high-intensity" cartridge generates great pressure in the chamber and strong breeches are needed.

The gun that did more than any other to harness the really high-speed cartridge was the Mauser bolt-action, an invention of the German, Peter Paul Mauser, some time before 1870. A bolt action was nothing new, the Dreyse needle gun having served well with it, but Mauser's bolt turned as it went forward or back. Its camming action was tremendously powerful and the lugs on the bolt itself formed tight lockup.

Its simplicity appealed to the world's armies, while seeming slow and awkward to sportsmen who had been brought up on the lever action

117

and were about to meet the semiautomatic. Although custom bolt-action sporters appeared almost immediately, it was more than sixty years before the bolt-action was widely accepted. By 1910 the bolt-action sporters of Europe had almost exactly the silhouette of the classic bolt rifles of 1970, except for the later provision of low telescopic sight mounting.

After the buffalo herds were gone a few sportsmen still preferred something more powerful than the thirty-thirty. Clinging to the big Sharps for some hunting, they became increasingly fond of the Remington rolling block and the heavier lever actions, such as the Winchester 95. Competitive levers, such as the excellent Marlin, appeared in a variety of cartridges. Although it may be that Marlin's design was partly accidental, the solid top of their rifle's action of 1893 had an advantage over Winchester, for it permitted low mounting of a telescopic

sight. Earlier models had ejected the empties upward, like the Winchesters.

One of the more popular of the black-powder cartridges was the .45-70, the American military cartridge through much of the Indian wars. It carried a large bullet and the rifles used for it were rugged, but the military turned strongly toward bolt actions with the Krag, adopted about 1892. It came from Norway as the Krag Jorgensen. The cartridge was the .30-40 or ".30 U. S.," and the rifle was one of the smoothest operating of any bolt action. However, its single locking lug was not satisfactory for the more powerful cartridges and its magazine required cartridges to be loaded one at a time.

The Mauser model of 1898 could be loaded from a clip for the military and is still accepted as the best bolt action type ever made, more recently altered for faster ignition.

118

After the Spanish-American War of 1898, Americans turned to the 1903 Springfield, a near-copy of the Mauser and loaded by a clip. Later gun authorities thought the original 1898 Mauser remained the better action. At the beginning of the century, military rifles were more important to the world's sportsmen than at any other time. It was the military cartridges that were the basis of most modern high-speed loads.

Sportsmen did not know how to judge bullets, however, and the world's armies were no help at all, for they began to use hard-jacketed projectiles for "humane" results. The heavily jacketed bullet did not cause as severe a wound as expanding ones and was piously used while chemists developed poison gases and artillery experts designed fiendishly effective explosive shells. And the sportsman did not understand.

He accepted the military cartridges and was astounded to find that some of them were poor killers on small European deer and thirty-five pound coyotes. Long after World War I there were riflemen who swore that the German 8mm Mauser and the American .30-06 were not powerful enough for deer. The hunter had omitted one part of the equation entirely. The hard-jacketed bullet delivered its power only when it met sufficient resistance. Rifles and calibers were blamed for bullet shortcomings.

Jacketed bullets were not necessary at relatively slow black-powder speeds but somewhere around fifteen hundred feet per second the ordinary lead bullet began to strip apart in the bore and its base melted. There were all sorts of "cups," and gas

119

checks or partial jackets, to avoid these problems, yet when the speed increased even more, the jacket became a difficult engineering task. Long before most hunters even thought of it, designers found that the perfect bullet's construction must be tailored to the size of animal it was intended for, the range at which it would be fired, and the way in which it struck the target. That, of course, was impossible—thus most bullets are compromises. Printed detail of these factors on a box of cartridges would cause the prospective purchaser to recoil, so the manufacturers promised rather general efficiency.

Thus careful marksmen stared in despair as their wounded eighty-pound pronghorn loped over the horizon, having shown little sign of being struck by the bullet that had felled a thousand-pound moose the week before. Generally, the rifle and caliber were blamed and such assessments have probably done more than anything else to foster the great number of cartridge types available in the past hundred years.

At first the bullet's jacket was mainly to protect the lead from the heat and pressure of smokeless powder. With increased speed its effect at the target became important. The term "controlled expansion" entered the bulletmaker's vocabulary.

The African hunter needed a solid bullet for penetration on elephants. Shooters of lighter game needed bullets that did not penetrate so deeply, yet expended their energy within the animal. So jackets were extended only part way, leaving some lead exposed at the point—a "soft-point bullet." The exposed lead was to expand, or spread, on impact,

and the remainder of the bullet was to hold its shape. It did or did not, depending upon its speed.

Thus began one of the most complex developments in the firearms industry. Bullets, which seemed a very simple part of the equation, stood in the way of practical use of high velocity.

As soon as smokeless powder increased bullet speed, the round-nosed or flat-nosed bullet was found inefficient at long range. A more streamlined shape was needed and the pointed, or "spitzer," bullet appeared, the name coming from Germany, where some of the most advanced development was under way. Eventually, for really long-range target shooting, there would be a "boat-tailed" bullet.

Long, exposed lead points were unsatisfactory. They were fragile in storage and battered badly within the rifle's magazine so that they were unbalanced. The tubular magazine so popular on lever-action rifles could not be used with any kind of pointed bullet, for the point of one cartridge rested against the primer of the one ahead of it.

The semipointed, hollow-point bullet, an early development, is still an efficient design for some purposes. The forward part of the metal jacket is left empty and there is a hole in the nose. On impact, the jacket pulls back and exposes the lead.

And jacket material was hard to choose and make. Soft steel served well on the "solids" for Africa. The mixture of copper and nickel, called German silver, had its day with expanding bullets. Much of the industry finally settled on gilding metal—a combination of copper and zinc. Mild steel has been a European favorite.

120

Cougar (far left) and coyote (left) have served as super-varmints. The coyote has been a target for some of the most advanced varmint shooters with the finest rifles. Hidden hunter (below) aims at one of the little wolves, a breed that has covered the United States. Lineup of Weatherby cartridges (bottom), fastest of factory loads, shows sharp shoulders, belted case.

Bullet failures have sometimes been spectacular for the researcher. There is the experimenter who assembles a high-speed cartridge with a lightly built bullet and finds no sign of a hole in his target. His bullet has disintegrated through its own speed of thrust and rotation.

To regulate the rate of bullet expansion, jackets have been built with varying thickness—thin near the point and thicker toward the base. Remington's Bronze Point has a bronze tip which protects the softer material from battering, then drives back into the lead body of the bullet to force expansion when the bullet strikes. In Winchester's Silvertip there is a material, different from the jacket's, which covers the point and extends to the bullet's base.

The German firm of DWM produced an "H-mantle" bullet with a thick belt inside the jacket itself, and the American, John Nosler, designed a similar bullet, a partition separating front and rear lead sections. The forward part opens easily and the base section, restricted by the heavy partition, is built to hold together.

Now that high velocity had been partly harnessed there were some close-range problems, and timber hunters spoke learnedly of a cartridge's "brush-busting" qualities. But it developed that only in extreme cases were there significant differences in brush-smashing qualities. If the bullet encountered resistance a considerable distance from its target, chances were it would be deflected regardless of caliber or speed.

The success or failure of the various modern cartridges has been almost completely un-

High-intensity big-game cartridge (right) goes into bolt-action where camming effect makes for tight lockup and accuracy. Ruger (opposite, front) and Browning singleshot (back) rifles are a touch of nostalgia and are recent introductions. Remington display (below) shows variety of types of modern ammunition.

predictable, some appearing to succeed under a new name when almost exactly the same cartridge failed in earlier introductions. Some have appeared two or even three times with mediocre success.

Sir Charles Ross introduced the 280 Ross in a rifle made in Quebec in 1906, and although the cartridge was excellent the rifle was a straight-pull bolt that proved unsatisfactory and even unsafe. Nevertheless, for a time the cartridge enjoyed considerable popularity, especially in England. Many years later Remington introduced the .280. It had similar ballistics, and although no critic could find real fault with it, only a few factory models were chambered for it and the list dwindled rapidly. The excellence of the 280 Remington is indicated by the number of custom rifles built for it—such guns are usually ordered by knowledgeable shooters. In this case the caliber must compete with the similar 270 Winchester, a commercial round of almost mystic attraction for the public. The 284 Winchester of similar ballistics has been coolly received.

Most modern cartridges began as "wildcats," even though some slight changes were made before they were built commercially. The term is applied to cartridges which have no commercial rifles available for their use. Usually they are constructed through alteration of an existing cartridge case. The Weatherby line of high-speed cartridges began as wildcats. Other examples include the .25-06, simply a .30-06 case altered to take a .25-caliber bullet instead of the .30-caliber one. Another is the .22-250, which began long ago as a wildcat, the Savage .250-3000 case necked down to take a .22 bullet.

Both became factory ammunition. Charles Newton, an American firearms expert, designed the first really fast .22 caliber—the 22 Hi-Power—which was used by Savage early in the century.

The most urgent quest for high velocity and innovation in cartridge design was not headed by big-game hunters in the wilds of desert, jungle, or mountains but by a new breed of gun lover, the American varmint shooter, who usually considered himself more of a rifleman than a hunter. His objective was a clean one-shot kill made through precise planning and generally at long range. His game, creatures that could be harmful to agriculture, were generally classified as "varmints."

His chosen word was "varmint," a variation of "vermin," although as the sport grew the targets gained so much of his respect that he was sometimes paradoxically engaged in protecting them from farmers who felt that judicious crop management or scientifically controlled poison could eliminate the problem once and for all. There are areas where varmint shooters have agreements with farmers in which they promise to keep the woodchuck population under control if the farmers will not eliminate them completely.

It was the eastern woodchuck that contributed most of all to the game. The shooter watched broad sweeps of green fields marked by occasional earthen mounds and hard-to-see den entrances, strategically arranged by chucks. To the shooter, riflery was a game of precision and he scorned nearby shots that might have been taken by a farm boy with a mail-order twenty-two. He became an addict of the

telescopic sight and the high-speed bullet, fast-moving for two reasons. First, only a swift bullet could hold a flat-enough trajectory to ensure hits on small targets. Secondly, the kill was made by the tremendous shock delivered by a thin-skinned projectile. Since the primary objective was the kill rather than meat for the table, near-total destruction of the target was desirable for it reduced the danger of crippling. Varmint bullets of later years could kill quickly, even when they did not strike what might be considered a vital area.

The bullets were largely of .22 caliber because they could be driven at high speed, and fast and frangible bullets were safe in settled communities because they disintegrated when they struck either chuck or ground. The cases were generally modifications of those made for larger bullets. So the varmint shooter often became a wildcatter and cartridges for use by another generation began in kitchens and toolsheds. The rifle continued its American development where it first began.

At intervals over the years, western big-game guides received surprises from the East. No, the tenderfoot would say, he did not want to follow elk into the tumbled brush of rocky canyons and he was not interested in confronting a grizzly on a high trail. He wanted to see the antelope; then he would unpack his heavy-barreled rifle with the bulbous telescope. The guide's task was simple, for this greenhorn did not need to get very close and often he bagged game that felt completely secure. While he did not often shoot his chuck rifle at pronghorns, he used a rifle and sight developed from woodchuck experience and he smiled at unending sweeps of sage with white-flecked targets hundreds of yards away.

There were other varmints besides the woodchuck or groundhog. The rockchuck, or marmot, was much like the eastern woodchuck and when the shooting was across a canyon the range might be even more difficult, so the western varmint shooter developed. There was the prairie dog, still a nuisance in some areas after it was considered a threatened species. There was the coyote, a sort of king of varmints, requiring careful hunting and marksmanship.

The earlier varmint shooters did not turn quickly to the bolt action, even though it had appeared about the time they began operations, nor were they satisfied with the ordinary sportsman's lever-action repeater or the new semiautomatics.

Their actions had to be stiff and rugged because pressures grew with high-speed smallbores and their need for accuracy was related to that of the old buffalo hunters. They turned largely to singleshot rifles, and since the old actions for large-bore ammunition did not fit well, there were a number of innovations.

Most singleshot actions were of falling-block design or modifications of it. The Stevens, Winchester, Remington-Hepburn, Sharps-Borchardt, and British Farquharson are well-known examples. Most had visible hammers, although the Sharps-Borchardt and the Farquharson did not. In 1883 the Winchester singleshot action was purchased from an inventor in Ogden, Utah. His name was John Moses Browning and Winchester paid $8,000.

The fast-traveling varmint bullets started a controversy—speed versus bullet weight—that continued spasmodically for almost a century, but the most successful cartridges were compromises.

There were millions of .22-rimfire cartridges made even before 1900 and the 22 Short was the first of the commercial, self-contained cartridges, introduced in 1857 by Smith & Wesson. The Long Rifle was in use by 1887.

Multiple millions of twenty-twos have been fired by beginning shooters, hairsplitting target riflemen, and millions of small-game hunters. Accepted early in its life as an efficient tool for tin cans, squirrels, rabbits, firearms instruction, and painstaking paper punching, it has been and remains the undisputed backbone of the firearms industry.

Some of the first twenty-twos were good enough to hold their own against all comers in

design. The Winchester repeating pump action of 1890 was built under a patent issued to John Browning and was made until 1932, with new guns supplied until 1941 with only slightly altered design. Its tubular magazine in the 22 Short model carried fifteen cartridges, an ample supply for those who fired fast at running game.

The semiautomatic Winchester 1903 model of the twenty-two was the first truly successful self-loading rifle of any kind and the same appearance was retained in a model that lasted until 1958.

But such twenty-twos and others of relatively expensive construction were a small fraction of the little rimfire rifles that Americans used. They have been made under long lists of names at prices as low as two dollars, and anyone who doubts their importance in the game fields must consider that the rabbit has been the leading game mammal in America for a century and more.

The twenty-two was a perfect cartridge for development of the self-loading rifle. It has slight recoil, does not develop extreme pressures, and works well in what gunmakers call the simple blowback system. That design features a breechblock held against the chamber by spring pressure; recoil of the cartridge moves the block backward, ejects the empty case, and brings a fresh cartridge into the chamber. Since the inertia of the movable block is an essential element, only light recoil could be handled. In other words, if the cartridge were very powerful the moving block would be too heavy for a shoulder gun. In some designs there were mechanisms built to "hold back" or restrain the block in its rearward travel. That is called the retarded blowback system.

There are other forms of self-loading that served in big-game rifles and shotguns. The short recoil system uses a breech bolt locked to the barrel and both barrel and bolt slide back together, compressing a recoil spring. After the bullet has left it the barrel stops and is unlatched from the bolt, which continues backward until it is stopped by a buffer; a spring then moves it forward again with a fresh cartridge. In the long-recoil system both barrel and breech recoil for a considerable distance and the breech is then held while the barrel is returned to its forward position by a spring. It extracts the empty case as it goes forward, then strikes a latch which releases the bolt so it comes forward with a loaded cartridge. In the gas system, a small quantity of gas from the fired cartridge is bled off from a hole in the barrel and is used to operate the mechanism. It was widely tried early in the game and was adopted only after other actions had long been used.

Winchester's first semiautomatic of deer caliber came in 1905 and looked very much like its first successful twenty-two. It was a retarded blowback and was poorly balanced for sporting use although widely used by law-enforcement agencies.

Appearing in 1906, a John Browning design for Remington, the Model 8, was more successful in deer forests. It was clumsy in appearance and rather heavy, since the entire recoiling barrel was enclosed in a spring and an outer tube. It re-

mained on the market for a long while and is still used considerably in whitetail deer country.

Until after World War I it was the military that stuck to the simplest actions and American hunters who sought rapid fire in lever, pump, and self-loading rifles. Back in the days of Indian wars there were complaints that the "savages" were likely to have repeaters against the singleshot, trapdoor Springfields. But the military abandoned the lever action after a brief trial and went to the bolt, while most hunters ignored it. After World War I, millions of Americans who had learned to use the bolt action in France began to consider it a sporting arm, much as Europeans did. And here American soldiers and civilians parted company, for the military moved toward semiautomatic and fully automatic guns.

It was 1921 before Remington introduced an American bolt-action sporter for big game. That was the Model 30, a remodeled, sporterized 1917 Enfield. Remington had built Enfield rifles for war use. Then Winchester introduced its Model 54 bolt in 1925.

These rifles followed bolt-action sporters made by custom gunsmiths for numerous prominent hunters, although at the time the custom rifle was not a particularly popular item. American connoisseurs were more interested in fine shotguns and regarded the rifle as a tool.

Two cartridges did much to convert American sportsmen to the bolt because no other action handled them as well. The .30-06, of course, now appeared in civilian dress with a variety of game bullets and more coming. The .270, made from

a necked-down .30-06 case, appeared for the new 54 rifle and was immediately accepted by those leaning toward lighter, faster bullets. Its 130-grain projectile had better sectional density than any similar weight for the .30-06 and remained a favorite. Jack O'Connor was an ardent supporter of the cartridge, advocating 150-grain bullets for some tasks, and he may have been the advocate who made it last, for the .270 remained a favorite half a century later.

One of the best balanced of the moderate- to high-velocity cartridges is the 7mm Mauser or 7 × 57mm, introduced in 1892. It served Spain, Mexico, and several South American countries as a military load and has been a truly international cartridge, although only modestly popular in the United States, where it has been handicapped by a limited variety of factory loads.

There were millions of inexpensive military actions scattered over the world and custom gunsmiths began to alter them to suit the hunter. They were more accurate than other repeaters and since they were adapted to long-range cartridges there was a quest for better sighting equipment in the form of adjustable peep and telescopic sights.

The telescopic sight caused changes in the rifle's design. The first telescopic sights had been long tubes, generally of considerable magnification but containing low light-gathering qualities, and some of them were as long as the rifle barrels themselves. They had been intended only for very deliberate use as in military sniping and there are reports that both sides used them during the American Revolution. Newer scopes had wider field, more eye re-

lief, and a greater light-gathering capacity. At first they were made principally in the optical centers of Europe; then American makers appeared too, and following World War II scopes were made in Japan.

Those earlier bolt actions had not been intended for use with telescopes and the bolt handles of most of them turned up over the breech, so that earlier hunting-scope mounts were quite high, making it almost impossible for a shooter to keep his cheek on the stock and still see through the eyepiece. For a time this was considered desirable as most shooters did not completely trust the scope. They felt it was fragile and easily knocked out of adjustment. They preferred having their rifles constructed primarily for iron sights close to the barrel.

When the scope was accepted as the most important aiming tool, gunsmiths began to alter actions to accept lower mounting, and at the same time the stocks were built straighter so the scope could be used naturally. There were all sorts of devices for quick removal of scopes and for swinging them out of the way. These devices remained for dangerous game but shortly after World War II confident users of scope sights for other purposes began to buy their rifles with no other sighting equipment.

Scopes became rugged and salesmen demonstrated some models by dropping them on concrete floors. It was some time before the problem of fogging was solved. There was disagreement concerning internal or external adjustments. Most of the large target scopes were adjusted from the outside until scope-sighting technology advanced sufficiently to permit internal adjustments. That is, the optics were adjusted rather than the alignment of the scope tube itself.

The all-around big-game scope settled somewhere around 4-power with less magnification needed for brush hunting and some big-game shooting done with 6-power. Then came the variable-power scope, slightly bulky for some purposes, yet good for a variety of others.

The telescope sight did not reach its heyday until the 1950s, but it was all-important in the development of precision ammunition. There was little use for a rifle that would put all of its bullets into a one-inch circle at one hundred yards if the average shooter could not hit a dishpan at that distance. With the telescopic sight he could hit a coffee cup. The varmint shooter had known this for a long time.

High velocity was relative. When Savage introduced its 250-3000 cartridge for the Model 99 lever rifle in 1915 it was sensational. The public had never used a big-game rifle that would drive a .25-caliber bullet at three thousand feet per second. It was and still is a fine deer cartridge. Few shooters then could aim well enough to take advantage of its capabilities.

With a high-velocity rifle, range judgment was less important (within reason) and there was a premium on careful holding. If his rifle were sighted in properly to begin with, a hunter could kill a deer at one hundred yards or at three hundred yards and aim at the same point for both ranges, an impossibility with a bullet that "dropped" several feet at that distance. With the telescopic sight, mod-

ern bolt actions, and good barrels, the stage was set for an enterprising American named Roy Weatherby. He came home from World War II and turned a whole family of high-speed wildcats into commercial cartridges. He put them into rifles with an appearance that appealed to much of the public and demonstrated their dramatic killing power—small, fast bullets against heavy game.

The three-thousand-feet-per-second line had been broken almost half a century before, but only dedicated rifle students paid much attention to it and the novelty had worn off. Weatherby's rifles often attained speeds of thirty-five hundred feet or more, and he went to Africa and proved that a bullet lighter than those of most deer cartridges could kill the biggest animals in the world. His concept was that if a bullet were driven fast enough it would kill anything, regardless of size.

Although many shooters would not go as far as Weatherby in their acceptance of high velocity, they wanted something that went faster than what they had been using. They bought the Weatherby rifles and they had other rifles chambered for the Weatherby cartridges. Weatherby had not only done well for himself but his concepts had caused the older firms to introduce similar cartridges. Typical examples were the 300 Norma Magnum, the 300 Winchester Magnum, and the 7mm Remington Magnum, very close in performance to Weatherby's 300 (best known of his line) and his 7mm. There was a long list of cartridges similar to the Weatherby line that were produced by various wildcatters but most of them lacked an established marketing outlet.

Shooting Flying

The shotgun's use is described as art, the rifleman's skill as science, although there is some of each in shooting either gun. And early development of the rifle closely followed the needs of war, whereas the fowling piece became a beloved possession invariably associated with the pleasures of hunting. Wingshooting has special significance, for "shooting flying" not only requires graceful skills but had its beginning as a sporting gesture, a deliberate handicap in many cases when the gunner could have more easily killed his game on the ground or on water. It was practiced early by the nobility when less favored hunters could not afford to pass up opportunities at sitting birds, the need for meat eclipsing any frivolous wishes for a sporting chance.

From the beginning there surely were attempts to hit moving targets, but efficient wingshooting was very difficult before the percussion cap. With the matchlock the lock time was terribly slow; it was greatly improved with the flintlock but the experts of shotgunning simply did not have the proper equipment until arrival of the percussion cap.

Wingshooting evidently began in France and Spain at about the same time, the lighter fowling pieces developing away from the concept of huge bores for flock shooting, although the market gunner's punt gun would be used centuries later.

Some of the most decorated guns were fowling pieces produced by French gunsmiths during the seventeenth century. Louis XIII, an avid collector of the period, had some two hundred and fifty of them. What is recognized as "the most valuable gun in the world" is an early flintlock built for the king in about 1615, when he was a youth. The builder was Pierre Le Bourgeoys of Lisieux. It was the peak time of ornate gun art in France, when some of the nobility's sporting arms were so heavily decorated that they were almost unrecognizable as guns.

But some French guns were practical and the best light fowling pieces were made there and in Italy. Britain's hold on the fine-gun market had not been established and, in fact, the English lagged far behind the French in wingshooting. They imported fine guns from France and Italy, and because of a pressing demand, some inferior ones, too.

One English writer, ruefully recognizing the French superiority in wingshooting, said in 1727: "I have often wondered why the French of all Mankind should alone be so expert at the Gun. I had almost said infallible. It's as rare for a profess'd Marksman of that Nation to miss a Bird as for one of Ours to kill. But, as I have been since informed they owe this Excellence to their Education. They are train'd up to it so very young, that they are no more surprized or alarm'd with a Pheasant than with a Rattle Mouse [bat]."

With wingshooting came the development of the pointing dog, perhaps no more important to the sporting scene than the trailing hound or the retriever, but a specialized animal whose performance related strongly to shooting flying. The "English pointer" evidently drew strongly from the hunting dogs of Portugal and Spain. The "English setter" appears to be an outgrowth of pointer and spaniel.

These bloodlines flowed back and forth through Spain, France, England, and other parts of Europe, following the fortunes of Europe's wars. In Germany there was more devotion to general-purpose dogs and the German pointing breeds of today are less specialized than the English products.

A mysterious contribution from France is the pointing Brittany spaniel, somewhat smaller than other pointers and said to have been a favorite of poachers. Very old pictures show dogs much like the modern Britt. After a long decline the breed was brought to a new height of development in the twentieth century.

When shotguns became lighter and faster swinging, there were artists who could perform marvels of marksmanship but in most cases they did not know how they did it and gave strange descriptions of their methods. Before much was known of the speed of shot as compared to that of the targets, there were marksmanship theories that began with superstition and approached fantasy.

It was strange that the first wingshooters hit anything at all, for there was an ongoing argument about the shot's speed, some expert gunners insisting there was no need for considering a time lag between gun and target. Richard Blome of Britain wrote about wingshooting late in the seventeenth century and touched a phase of the subject that confused gunners for centuries. His words are similar to those in sporting magazines of a much later date: "Some are of the Opinion that you must shoot something before the Fowl otherwise it will be past before the Shot can come to it; but this is a vulgar Error, for no Game can fly so quick, but that the Shot will meet it; for the Shot flyeth as wide as about the Compass of a Bushel, if rightly order'd in the Charging."

In an advanced age, when shot speeds and target speeds had been effectively measured, it was known that a crossing bird might move more than twenty feet after the shooter willed his finger to press the trigger. Yet shooters who refused to "lead," as the Americans say, or give "forward allowance," as the British say, continued to hit game. In the 1920s there was still argument in outdoor magazines as to how far ahead a marksman should shoot at a crossing bird. With later timing devices it was easy to arrive at the figures, but the way an expert placed the muzzle at that distance ahead of his target was indescribable for the expert himself, who often swore that he shot at the bird's beak, even if he stood at right angles to it. Then mathematicians would explain that such could not be the case, but they had no dead birds with which to prove their argument.

The lead compensation is handled by the shooter's subconscious; theoretically, he last sees the gun at the bird's beak. When it is discharged, it must be farther ahead or he would miss.

But the aura of mystery that has always surrounded expert shotgunnery was a help to its popularity rather than a hindrance, for the subtleties of gun design have engrossed generations of shooters and still lead to the costly manipulation of minute stock measurements and barrel lengths. The true artist must have the proper tools.

The French not only excelled the British in wingshooting for many years, producing some of

SHOOTING FLYING

the best early light fowling pieces, but they were leaders in development of modern breechloading shotguns. Johannes Samuel Pauly had a break-open breechloader firing a cardboard case in 1812 and Casimer Lefaucheux brought forth his double-barreled shotgun with a pinfire cartridge in 1835. The pinfire cartridge was used long after later types of primers were developed.

So the French led the world with what began to look very much like a modern British double, but the British were busy, too, and learned shooting flying themselves. The sleek, hammerless, side-by-side double actually got its start with Anson and Deeley, who were employed by Westley Richards in London. Their principles, as involved in 1875 patents, have been used with minor changes ever since, and long after their patents expired their names are still freely used by other makers.

An exceptional double-barreled shotgun design, first produced in France before 1900, has continued to be popular there but has had much less use in other parts of the world. It is the Darne, which under other circumstances might have been the world standard instead of the break-open British double. English guns caught the eye of an immense American market.

Instead of breaking for loading or unloading, the Darne has a receiver which slides straight back, operated by "ears" (or handles) ahead of the "wrist" (or grip). It is a simple extraction system, extremely powerful, and lends itself to light gun construction. Highly complimented by the world's gun critics and noted for its efficient handling of

misshapen or swollen cartridges, the Darne's design allows the breech to be fitted precisely against the cartridges, an added safety margin.

Although the Darne gun (built at St. Etienne, possibly the world's oldest center of gun manufacture) might be more adaptable to mass production than other double-barrel actions, it has traditionally been made with a great deal of handwork, many of them on a custom basis.

American and European objectives were different. By the latter part of the nineteenth century most of Europe had adopted the system of driven game. It was a gentleman's form of sport, based on the presence of numerous helpers, and its traditions became so formalized that most of them have been retained for more than a century. Grouse, pheasant, and partridge are the best-known targets, although the drives work for hares and other small game. With modifications they also work for deer and boar.

European game, raised as a crop, is the property of the landowner, whereas wild American game is considered public property, regardless of where it is found. The British shoot is traditionally a social affair with the "guns" taking position at numbered blinds, or butts, sometimes permanent stands which have been used by generations of tweed-clad sportsmen. Drivers, or beaters, move the game to the shooters.

The truly formal arrangement includes one gun in each butt, assisted by a loader. The fully equipped British shooter uses a matched pair of doubles, often with gold inlaid numbers to distinguish them, and the loader is in charge of keeping the arms loaded and ready to use.

In a polished series of precise movements, the loader receives the gun that has been discharged, replacing it with the fully loaded one from his position a little behind and to one side of the gunner. The loader often carries a shell bag with special clips for individual cartridges so that they can be inserted instantly.

Much of the game is taken coming into the butts or after it has passed and is going away, a matter which has had some bearing on gun design. The supreme achievement of the stand shooter is to kill two incoming birds from a flock and then two more outgoing after changing guns. In many instances there is no firing at birds far to the right or left because of danger to other shooters.

Some of the finest shots in the world have been produced by driven game and Americans who scorned such "contrived" shooting have been humbled in their first experience at facing birds hurtling over a hedge or line of trees at low altitude.

According to Percy Stanbury, a respected British shooting instructor: "One kill to two cartridges throughout the day is good shooting but one in three is more likely throughout the season; one in four is quite satisfactory for the average shot. The first-class shot, of whom there are remarkably few, probably averages about seventy kills to a hundred cartridges during a whole season."

In England it is called "rough shooting," but a majority of American hunters walk for their upland game, and although there is a great deal of that done by the British and other Europeans,

their best guns have been designed less for that than for formal shooting. To begin with, Americans have considered their shotguns as tools, rather than as showpieces or family treasures. Only a few of the wealthier Americans have been interested in the precision workmanship of British guns. The fact is that plain guns with less critical tolerances and the simplest mechanisms had an advantage in the New England grouse thickets or the Mississippi River swamps.

A market hunter tended to work with basics as much as possible. Sometimes he was unable to give his gun a thorough, regular cleaning. Certainly he was unable to return it annually to the maker for a thorough going-over in the English tradition. It was a great advantage for him to be able to disassemble it himself with simple tools, and he had little desire for delicate engraving or a breech that would not close on a grass seed. So the American gun builders really had two objectives: to please the vast majority of their customers, who wanted plain, serviceable guns at a low price; and to satisfy those few willing to pay for something that could compete with British quality.

Even before the assembly line was truly established, American builders were relying more and more on machines for operations done by hand in England and the continent. American preferences for repeaters led later on to the manufacture of such guns in Europe, especially in Belgium, France, and Italy, many of them aimed at the American market.

In 1881, W. W. Greener, a respected sage of the British firearms industry, scathingly denounced American gun builders in *The Gun and Its*

One of the most valuable shotguns in the world is this highly decorated "Napoleon" model by the French gunmaker Boutet. It is doubted if it was actually made for the emperor. Originally a flintlock, it was equipped with percussion locks (far right). French were leaders in lush decoration.

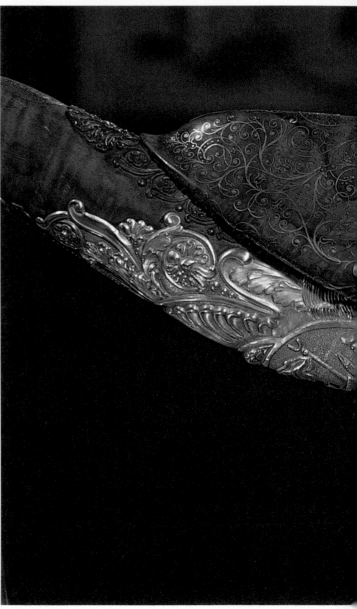

Development. After a detailed and bitter description of shoddy American manufacturing, he concluded with: "In fact, the shooting arm produced by scheme and human machines calling for no thought or skill on the part of the maker is hardly useful or sound. No public proofhouse exists in the United States, and to the American sportsman is the proving of the guns entrusted."

As the time of the repeater approached in the late nineteenth century, the American market for inexpensive guns was served by English and Belgian builders, as well as by Americans. These very plain and sometimes cheaply constructed shotguns came with many names, some of them using the trademarks similar to those of companies noted for a much higher class of merchandise. Some of the names were almost the same as those of famous builders with only the spelling slightly changed. America's devotion to machine work, sometimes done with less-than-painstaking care, was appearing in other countries.

In the last thirty years of the century there was a great number of American manufacturers of shotguns, most of the best-quality guns being made by Baker, Colt, Fox, Ithaca, Hunter Arms Company (L. C. Smith), Lefever, Parker, and Remington.

Europeans tended toward lighter guns; Americans have never been critical of shotgun weight. European loads have been lighter than American charges, making it possible to use the lighter guns without suffering from recoil. Europeans also have a completely different concept in gun mounting from that of Americans, one that is seldom

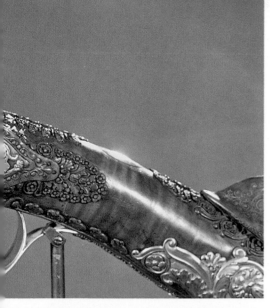

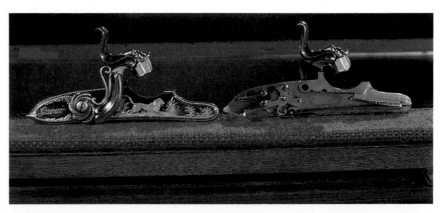

mentioned in discussions of weight and balance.

The usual British system for mounting and firing is based on fine gun fit. The British instructor tells his pupil to watch the speeding target and to ignore the appearance of his sight or gun muzzle. As the gun is being mounted, the muzzles—meaning the side-by-side double guns the British generally use—track the target, and at the instant the butt strikes the shoulder the gunner fires. In theory, the muzzles will follow the game as the shooter's eye does, a sort of instinctive shooting, much like pointing a finger. Many users of that system actually do point a finger of the hand that supports the barrels, and here is the chief difference between the British system and that of most Americans, for the English gets its momentum by having the arm swing with the guiding hand far out along the barrels.

In fact, the artfully checkered fore end of the typical European gun is generally very slender and the hand actually grasps the barrels completely above it toward the muzzles. For convenience, many shooters use a hand guard for clamping to the barrels and the instructor may say that "the fore end is to hold the gun together, not for use while firing."

Thus the speed of the barrel's sweep is actually a matter of arm swinging. The American method involves holding the fore end hand closer to the receiver, or breech, and the muzzle's weight is what causes the swing to accelerate. American instructors will tell clay-target shooters that the closer the hand is to the receiver the faster the muzzle will move, a matter of leverage. Fred Missildine, a dean of American shooting instructors, says: "It is possible to become a good shot in spite of the fault [extending the arm], but not a great one."

The British, of course, preach this "fault" and hit with it. Such conflicting concepts are not totally a matter of geography, but they persist on both sides of the Atlantic to this day.

Americans were primarily a "nation of riflemen" and approached their shotguns from the rifleman's viewpoint. Even though there were many years of double-barreled guns before the repeater appeared, it was accepted partly because the single barrel appeared to be capable of more careful pointing, and the word "aiming" was used rather than precise sighting. The relatively muzzle-heavy repeater adapted to the American style.

140

There was a feeling in Europe, shared in the United States by many sportsmen, that the repeater took unfair advantage of game and that two shots should be enough for any gunner. But here the British shooter showed a willingness to use a loader and two shotguns to be passed back and forth with practiced precision, thus being able to fire an almost endless series of shots in rapid succession.

While the merits of the two types of guns offset each other, the insistence of the double-gun lover brought about some of the most precise workmanship ever applied to any mechanism. The demand for repeaters was a factor in the development of mass production.

Despite their deceptively uncomplicated appearance, fine double-barreled guns are most difficult of all sporting arms to build. The "best" grades of British shotguns and the double rifles that have accompanied them have been made as individual projects with a minimum of machine work and by lifetime craftsmen who may have "worn a hole in the floor at the bench," as an executive of a London gun firm put it. The vagaries of currency fluctuations make it difficult to pin the dollar value, but the finest of British shotguns with standard decoration cost more in 1978 than a luxury-model American automobile. The best Italian, Spanish, Belgian, and German guns are somewhat less expensive.

The value of British firearms is gauged by the precision of their construction and the fine woods and selected metals of which they are made. Their efficiency in use may be no more than that of moderately priced guns, and their durability may be no greater, but the "best" guns have a tradition of faultless workmanship, much of which is invisible to the user and some of which has no bearing on operation. So the cost of production is there.

The very nature of repeating guns makes some precision impossible, for considerable tolerance is necessary or repeating actions simply will not work. Repeaters which demand handwork have been unable to compete with those produced almost entirely by machines. The buyer of repeating shotguns, regardless of his desire for engraving, inlays, or fine woods, purchases a mass-produced mechanism with replaceable parts. A "best" double gun is one of a kind in nearly all of its components.

Most of the fine American double shotguns had their beginnings before the pumpgun truly arrived, and that date can be set around 1900 with the popularity of Winchester's Model 1897, a pumpgun still in use by many hunters and sold for many years in various forms, even after it competed with the Winchester Model 1912 and highly efficient guns by Marlin, Remington, and others.

Even as a few Europeans chose to use "magazine guns," some Americans clung to fine doubles and bought handworked models turned out from special benches in mass-producing factories. The best known of the high-grade American guns was the Parker, often said to have been the finest of all, although some of its fame is due to its popularity with collectors, encouraged by gun writers.

The company from which the Parker gun emerged built rifles for the Union army during the Civil War and converted to production of sport-

Three of the most prestigious
names in firearms appear on
classic doubles (opposite).
Left to right are: a W. & C.
Scott 20 gauge, a Westley-
Richards twelve and a Holland
& Holland in the 10-gauge Royal
model. In details of breech
sections (below), delicate
engraving is typical of
British tradition.

ing guns shortly afterward, the first Parker shotguns going on sale in 1868. The Parker appeared as a hammerless in 1889 and the automatic ejector (ejecting fired cartridges upon opening) was introduced in 1902. Other developments included the single-trigger mechanism by 1922; the broad "beavertail" fore end, an American design, in 1923; and the raised and ventilated rib for the double in 1926. Other companies used these features beginning about the same time. The single trigger, beavertail fore end, and ventilated rib were not widely accepted abroad and became identified with American guns. They are still the subject of discourses by European gun writers, most of whom minimize their worth.

The Parker Brothers company was purchased by Remington in 1934 and the guns were produced until World War II, when most high-grade American doubles were discontinued. The basic Parker design was the boxlock, a less expensive mechanism to produce, in most cases, than the sidelock.

The well-known L. C. Smith was a sidelock and Lefever Arms sidelocks were popular in the higher grades. The majority of the British "best" guns have been sidelocks. The expensive and customized Winchester Model 21, still being made, is a boxlock. When both design and workmanship are good, arguments about the relative merits of box- and sidelocks are academic.

The pumpgunner of American marshes and uplands, although at first snubbed as a game hog by many Americans and long scorned by gentlemen sportsmen of other countries, became an artist in his own right. His heyday came with the twentieth century, and although semiautomatic guns developed along with the "trombone" mechanism he still retained pride in its operation after nearly a hundred years.

A Spencer model of 1885, based on an 1882 patent, is usually considered the first really successful pumpgun, although there had been efforts in that direction since before the Civil War. The Burgess pumpgun of late in the century involved sliding the grip instead of the forearm, but the trombone action was the one that stayed. Pumpgun believers insist they can fire properly pointed shots as fast or faster than users of semiautomatics or doubles. Certainly the best of them can.

After the first pumps, competition from semiautomatics was not long in coming, for a Browning patent of 1900 produced the "humpbacked" model, famous for years as built by the Browning company and by Remington, and still being produced in the same silhouette. Semiautomatics be-

came more streamlined in appearance after World War II, even while retaining the long-recoil system of the original Browning. The original design with the rear of the receiver vertical resulted in the shooter holding his head fairly erect and amounted to increased stock "drop." Generations of hunters learned to insist on this "hump."

It was gas operation that took the American public's eye in the 1950s with Remington as the leader, and out of it came the Remington 1100, destined to be one of the more popular shotguns of all time, and able to back its popularity with successes in competitive shotgun sports, both trap and skeet. Gas operation of automatic weapons had been around since before 1900, but the principle had not been effectively applied to sporting guns. Wayne Leek headed work in designing the 1100. Other manufacturers in America, Japan, and Europe eventually made similar guns, but the Remington model had a long head start in popularity.

In effect, the gas system prolongs the gun's kick so that it becomes a shove rather than a blow, and the tired trap or skeet competitor, confronted by the physical and mental shocks of hundreds of shots on the same day, has often welcomed the aid of reduced recoil.

The variety in American shotgunning has done much to foster variety in guns generally and strong opinions about them, and while many American sportsmen smile at the formality of European sport there is traditional American shooting as well. The quail plantation is an institution of the American South, requiring its own formal approach, different from any other form of upland gunning. There the double gun is king, usually in 20 gauge.

For many years the trend has been toward smaller bores in shotguns, and while the 10 gauge was very nearly an "average" at one time, the 12-gauge gun has far outstripped every other for general use. The 16 gauge has been continuously popular on the European continent but has lost much of its sale in America. The English gun is predominately 12 gauge, although often very light in weight and firing only light charges. English duck guns, intended for heavy charges, more nearly approach American weights.

Gauges have been standardized. At one time there were dozens, making ammunition production impossibly complex. The 10 gauge is usually found only where long-range shooting is done at large birds. The 12 gauge is the standard and is used for everything with the industry's widest variety of loads. The 20 gauge is gaining popularity, although

chiefly as an upland gun. The 28 gauge has been kept alive largely through the demands of formal skeet shooting, although it produces remarkable results for cartridge-design reasons. The .410 is a part of the skeet program and is used in only specialized forms of game shooting.

For some time it has been predicted that the 20 gauge will replace the 12 gauge as the 12 replaced an assortment of larger bores, but the small-bore shotgun, even though it may fire the same amount of shot, has inherent difficulties producing effective patterns. Whenever the shot column becomes excessively long, as is the case with heavy loads in a smallbore barrel, the patterns suffer because of excessive shot deformation. Shot is deformed not only by its contact with the barrel on the way out, but by the crushing pressure of the powder's gases at its base.

Shot and its performance has been one of the most difficult studies of the gun designer's craft. The muzzleloader of Fred Kimble's day actually had some advantages over the modern shotgun because his gun was of large bore for the amount of shot it fired. An 8-bore gun of that day would probably throw less shot than a heavily loaded 12-gauge gun of today, thus preventing the pellets from crushing each other so badly. And the muzzleloader was not involved with the complexities of forcing cones located in the barrel ahead of modern cartridges.

Most shot, despite various modifications of method, has been made by droplets of melted lead falling for a considerable distance in "shot towers" and becoming near-perfect spheres

when they strike water far below. "Chilled" shot got its name from fast cooling done as the shot was falling, causing it to harden.

Some upland gunners firing close range at ruffed grouse, quail, and woodcock, misinterpreted the results of soft shot. Their increased success with it was due to fast-opening patterns that scattered at close range and felled the birds that were missed by harder shot which went forth in a smaller pattern. Wildfowl shooters, however, rightly claimed that at long range the harder shot was superior. The truth was that many upland gunners bagged their game with deformed pellets which behaved erratically and "opened" the pattern.

Today, while virtually all shot is hardened by the inclusion of some material other than lead, most of it is still soft enough to be affected greatly by deformation within the gun, and deformation gives a result that demands explanation. The charge of shot travels in a formation that becomes funnel-shaped rather than cone-shaped. As the charge emerges even badly deformed pellets are controlled by the choke or muzzle size for a short distance. They lose speed faster than round pellets, however; they begin to diverge as their initial velocity is lost and they turn outside the main pattern. By thirty or so yards many of these deformed pellets are so far from the point of aim that they do not even appear on the testing target. The smaller the bore the more of the shot is affected by crushing and "barrel scrub," and the harder it is to maintain a good pattern.

The smallbore shotgun was given an enormous assist by the "sleeve wad," or "shot col-

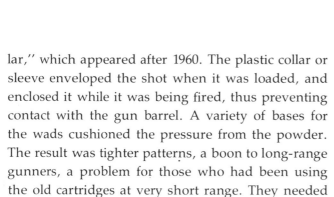

A Remington pumpgun, Model 17 (top), carries extensive factory engraving. Three of America's best-known doubles (below) appear in the better grades. From top is 12-gauge Fox; Winchester Model 21, still built as a custom item; an Ithaca 12 gauge, engraved at factory. All are boxlocks.

lar,'' which appeared after 1960. The plastic collar or sleeve enveloped the shot when it was loaded, and enclosed it while it was being fired, thus preventing contact with the gun barrel. A variety of bases for the wads cushioned the pressure from the powder. The result was tighter patterns, a boon to long-range gunners, a problem for those who had been using the old cartridges at very short range. They needed more open bores.

Although thousands of booted wild-fowlers with magnum repeaters may face bitter winds on a thousand dawns over ice-trimmed marshes, and thousands of briar-scratched grouse seekers may swing their short-barreled favorites at fleeting glimpses, their results are hard to evaluate. Practical capabilities of shooting equipment are generally appraised in competition of one kind or another, even though conditions are not precisely the same as in the field. By the twentieth century competitive shotgunning was becoming well organized.

But flintlock, and perhaps even matchlock shooters, had competed in Europe long before that. There was a great deal of money bet on results at driven game, especially on the continent, and evidently in preparation for such events the trapped-pigeon shoot became popular in England. Various kinds of pigeons were released in a variety of ways before the American Revolution, and pigeon shooting, with some modern embellishments, has continued to the present time, still involving a great deal of money.

The Old Hats of England received their name some time after 1800 because birds were con-

150

cealed under hats until the release signal. There were many other pigeon clubs, as well. Basically, the game has been to kill the released bird before it crosses a line or barrier. Illegal in some places, it is still regarded as a peak in shotgun competition.

There are two distinct forms of competitive live-pigeon shooting. In one the pigeons are thrown by hand into the air, the thrower being highly skilled at the more important shoots. The bird must be killed before it escapes from a hundred-meter scoring ring. The competitor is allowed two shots. In the other form of shooting the gunner faces a row of traps or boxes, not knowing which one will release a bird. Upon his command the trap is opened and he has two shots with which to kill the bird before it crosses a low fence seventeen and a half yards from the trap. The bird must fall within the fence and if it lands outside it is scored as a miss.

Much depends on the kind of pigeons used. When live-pigeon matches began in America long before the Civil War, passenger pigeons were plentiful. They were the basis of live-bird shooting until they were nearly gone some time late in the century. Ordinary "domestic" pigeons are widely used, generally a mixture of breeds and of highly varied flight qualities. In Britain, the shooters used the wood pigeon and then the more agile blue rock pigeon, but the most respected of all is the Spanish pigeon or *zurito*. Spain remains one of the more important of the pigeon-shooting countries, attracting gunners from around the world.

The details of pigeon shooting are especially important in gun design, for the arms used are chosen for their ability to kill game with precision, with little regard to cost. Until recent years, the side-by-side double had been the most popular "live-bird" gun. Today its place is being taken by the over-under.

Inanimate objects fired at by shotgunners included various metal "birds" and glass balls, sometimes filled with feathers, but "clay pigeons," much as used today, became the standard before 1900. Actually, they are primarily composed of pitch.

The United States has its own formal clay-target trapshooting, a game that has steadfastly held much the same form for nearly a century. Skeet is a more recent sport. It has fewer followers, most of them—as with trapshooting—in the United States. There are international forms of both games, enough different from American competition to provide another set of champions.

As hunting receded farther and farther from the large centers of population there was more demand in America for shooting grounds easily and quickly reached. The skeet or trap club has filled that gap to an increasing extent.

Since their sport has never attracted many spectators, the clay-target shooters have been largely an unseen group. A large share of the shotgun ammunition used in the United States is fired at clay targets, an estimated 800 million shots per year.

The shotgun games that were originated as practice for game shooting have invariably developed into ends in themselves and attract the world's best marksmen, many of whom never hunt. They use some of the finest guns of all.

153

7

Matters of Opinion

Some sporting guns have been sold in almost the same form for nearly a century, yet thousands of models have come and gone in that time. Many new ones are introduced each year, most of them soon to disappear. Of course, there have been inferior designs and unneeded calibers, but efficiency or durability have not been the sole reasons for what seems to be the sportsman's fickle regard for new models. The largest manufacturers, using the most modern market surveys, have had spectacular failures with new guns, some of which performed well.

The conclusion is that gun users make their choices in ill-defined ways as mysterious as the style choices for automobile or clothing buyers. In competitive target shooting, whether with bullet or shot, there are at least measurable objectives to be achieved. In hunting, the personal choice is frequently strongly defended by a shooter who has never even tried a different kind of gun.

Most mysterious of all is the matter of gun appearance. Disagreements as to what a gun should look like can be violent. While nearly all published gun experts insist that the most attractive shotgun is the light side-by-side double, there are shooters who will insist that a gun with two barrels must be extremely clumsy and very heavy, when actually some of the lightest and fastest-handling guns are doubles.

Others bewail the mechanical ugliness of magazine repeaters, yet someone recently wrote to a gun publication that of all the world's shotguns, the Model 12 Winchester pump was the most attractive to look at.

Bolt-action rifles were considered supremely ugly by most sportsmen before the military models were "sporterized" by custom gunsmiths. Now most gun writers consider the "classic bolt" a thing of beauty, an art form in itself. There are others who prefer the "California school" of bolt-action stocking, a form that has sometimes gone to radical shapes, certainly much more showy than the classic rifle. Any lover of artistic gun design must agree that the rakishly designed gun with inlays, bright spacers, and sweepingly different stock is invariably chosen as the most valuable by anyone inexperienced in firearms. The lover of conservative design is forced to the lame explanation that there must be knowledge of art before it can be appreciated.

The lever-action rifle with full-length magazine owes millions of its sales to Hollywood, for fifty years of motion-picture frontiersmen have carried it. Adult users of such rifles and carbines are reluctant to confess that one of their main reasons for buying them was the reflection of Hollywood glamour.

The single-action revolver, featured in thousands of Western motion pictures, television shows, magazines, and novels, was hopelessly outdated by 1940 in the opinion of most lawmen, serious target shooters, and hunters. When production was discontinued the old guns leaped in value and new and improved models were introduced by several manufacturers—all carefully retaining the silhouette of the old Colt "Peacemaker." They sold well and are still being sought by hunters. For years there was a quick-draw craze that swept the country and produced hundreds of clubs where shooters competed against electric timers, using single-action guns. Doubtless many of those competitors have been faster than the gunfighters they mimicked.

Thousands of costumed "buckskinners" go back to the ways of mountain men and use flintlock and percussion guns built in modern factories. So the appeal of guns is sometimes hard to predict, being part efficiency, part tradition, and not a little fantasy. The number of gun models and cartridges built and used shows that there are sure to be strong differences of opinion, some of which can never be resolved. These differences are frequently between experts in the field, and some have provided running arguments for almost a century.

Possibly the longest and steadiest disagreement has concerned the double-barreled shotgun versus the repeater. The repeater has certainly been the leader in the United States and the double has never lost its supremacy in Europe. It all began around 1900, when the 1897 Winchester pump ("Old Cornsheller") established its popularity. For some time many Americans were violently opposed to repeaters, but most of their criticism soon died out. Repeaters did not push quality doubles out of American factories until World War II.

British shooters, however, were bitterly opposed to "magazine guns" and most of them have remained so. When Americans began to buy over-under shotguns in great numbers, British gun writers considered that little better than the pumps and automatics, and wrote a great many words explaining the superiority of side-by-side barrels.

Since John Browning somehow seemed to invent the repeating shotgun almost singlehandedly, he is blamed by Gough Thomas, the British gun authority, for inflicting permanent damage on the shotgunning tradition. After telling of the goals of fine gunmaking, Thomas (G. T. Garwood in real life, writing in *Gun Digest*, 1967) says: "Browning had nothing in common with these gunmakers or their ideals. With the nineteenth century market gunner obviously in mind, his aim was clearly a high-firepower weapon capable of being cheaply mass-produced by machinery. By ignoring the demands of elegance, he was able to adopt the forward, tubular magazine and slide action. If the latter was admirably convenient, it nevertheless entailed a long receiver and a forward redistribution of weight which sacrificed . . . everything that gunmakers had done to improve the balance, liveliness and fast-handling quality of the sporting gun since Henry Nock's patent breech of the 1780s had cut 6 to 10 inches off the flintlock barrel and made double guns a feasible proposition. . . . Browning debased the gunmaker's craft and introduced an inflexibility which has acted as a great bar to the progressive development hitherto associated with these weapons."

The user of the repeater had more firepower at his disposal, but there were other reasons why it prospered in America. Interchangeable parts became a part of the American scheme of things before they were valued elsewhere, and the repeater was perfect for machine-made parts that would have

required hand-fitting for double guns, and most of all for the precision arms of Britain.

European shotguns had their own silhouettes, generally more graceful than those of American doubles, partly because of tradition. The British drill of shooting with the forward arm extended placed little importance on the fore end as a handle, so it continued to appear as what Americans called a "splinter."

Then, since the British and sportsmen of continental Europe were strong believers in double triggers for instant barrel selection, they generally have preferred a "straight" stock without what shooters call a "pistol grip." The theory is that the straight grip makes hand shifting easier and is helpful in manipulating double triggers. Beyond that there is another reason, tied to game-shooting form. Natural pointing is best achieved with the hands held in about the same plane, and with the "splinter" fore end the front hand tends to be above one that holds a pistol grip.

For a time the "beavertail" or "semibeavertail" fore end, a blocky wooden handle under the barrel built by Americans, was ridiculed by gunners of other countries. Its purpose nonetheless was a sensible one: to put the forward hand in line with the stock hand. It added a bulky appearance to the gun with its already bulging pistol grip but was ideal for the American style of shooting.

When smokeless powder reduced the importance of barrel length (black powder required more burning room) it took most of the shotgun fraternity almost a hundred years to conclude that extra barrel length did not necessarily mean a worthwhile increase in velocity. Some casual shooters never did recognize it.

But barrel length brought on a verbal battle that continued in Britain and on the continent for fifty years, this time with Americans playing little part. It began in the 1920s when Robert Churchill introduced twenty-five-inch barrels on fine English shotguns. They were three to five inches shorter than most of the best English guns, and European gun writers of the time leaped into the controversy. Such guns, opponents insisted, did not point well and looked strange, especially when used by tall men. "Sighting radius" was necessary for accuracy, they insisted.

Churchill had a special design in addition to the short barrel: the "Churchill rib," so constructed and tapered as to give the illusion of length as the shooter looked down it. From the shooter's end, proponents said, no one could tell that the gun was shorter, and the short barrel was handier and faster. The Churchill barrel length became such an issue that his guns were nicknamed in Roman numerals, simply as the "XXV."

Then, with all the argument, it began to be a magic figure, although it was no critical measurement, no better in a given situation than twenty-four or twenty-six inches. Fifty years after the great

debate started, shooters ordering custom guns would simply say, "Make it twenty-five inches, like the Churchill."

In the twentieth century barrel lengths somehow became standardized, and those who were the originators or imitators will never be known. The twenty-five-inch barrel remained a bit uncommon over most of the world and the standard became thirty inches for tightly choked guns, twenty-eight inches for less choke, and twenty-six inches for open-bored arms. Illogically, the lengths held for all types of actions.

A repeater with a twenty-six-inch barrel would be as long or longer overall than a double-barreled gun with a thirty-inch barrel, with the attendant features of balance, but a twenty-two-inch repeater barrel or a thirty-four-inch double barrel is unusual indeed in hunting guns. Since differences in actual performance are minuscule, there is neither justification nor defense for barrel lengths. Like left-hand handkerchief pockets, the fashion is unassailable the world over.

And the rib, or the sighting plane, for shotguns, became something of an American tour de force. Since many Americans liked the tradition of the British side-by-side shotgun but preferred a single sighting plane, they set their ribs high above the barrels and the ventilated rib became an American feature, no matter who first invented it.

Now it became the English against the Americans again, the Americans self-consciously quiet about their single sighting plane, while English experts railed against it as a rifleman's gadget and printed innumerable pictures to prove that the side-by-side double was more visible without the high rib and that two barrels led the eye to the target naturally. The ventilated rib did help prevent heat waves from disturbing the pointing picture when firing was rapid, and the Americans must have won this debate for the world turned to ventilated ribs, especially in competitive shotguns used to shoot for money—a difficult situation to disregard.

When the over-under shotgun began to become popular in the 1920s it was regarded as little short of scandalous by some traditionalists. It was not new. In fact, some of the earliest double-barreled guns had been built with one barrel atop the other,

but the design had faded with the appearance of smokeless powder.

One gun probably did more than anything else to popularize the over-under. This was the Browning Superposed, which began its career at about the time of John Browning's death in the twenties. It was made in Belgium and became a leading model the world over, selling in the upper-middle price range. It was the standard over-under until the late 1970s when Belgian production costs priced it out of the market and the Browning company crossed the world to Japanese factories, although still producing a few high-grade Superposeds. If its mechanism was a bit complex, it was nonetheless the unchallenged leader in sales for many years.

The faults of the over-under were its resistance to side winds, its bulky appearance, its extra cost, its tendency toward more weight, and the necessity for breaking it deeply to extract or load. Its advantages were that it recoiled straight back and that the lower barrel was set so far that its discharge did not disturb the pointing as much as did a side-by-side discharge.

The Americans, who had economized with repeaters, thus showed a preference for the most costly design of all. British makers, who produced "under-overs," found themselves competing with continental builders and some Americans. The plant that made the British Woodward, one of the finest of all, was destroyed during World War II.

It became difficult to speak ill of the over-under, for by the seventies it was chosen the competitor in international tournaments at skeet,

*Turkey hunters argue merits
of rifle versus shotgun,
but all are students of
call and camouflage. Hunter
on stand (below) uses box
call as in closeup (right).
Autoloading shotgun rests
across knees. The moment
of impact is dramatized
(opposite) as game is
struck by fatal shot.*

clay target, and live pigeon, and it had a large share of the market on American skeet and trap fields. Its competitor at American skeet was the gas-operated semiautomatic, chosen for its soft recoil.

It was on the continent that the "drilling," a gun of two or more calibers or gauges, became popular. A common arrangement was two shotgun barrels, side by side, with a rifle barrel beneath them. Some of the world's finest workmanship has gone into these guns and they have been especially popular in Germany and Austria. Continental Europeans have habitually hunted for a mixed bag.

A shotgun-rifle combination seems an excellent choice for a grouse hunter who might encounter deer, bear, or wild hogs; still, Americans have not taken to it, except in turkey hunting, where a shooter might use a rifle for a standing shot and keep his shotgun barrel for a bird that runs or flies. There have been fairly inexpensive combination guns made for that in America. The finer models usually come from Germany, Austria, or Belgium.

It was a favor to the world's shooters when shotgun gauges became standardized. While gauges have become fewer, the list of rifle cartridges has lengthened endlessly, a complexity for one who must buy ammunition in the far places, and the list still grows.

The standardization of shotgun gauges has been dramatic. Best known the world over is the 12 gauge, with ammunition available almost everywhere shotgun game is to be found. This gauge gained its popularity as smokeless powder took over and its acceptance was largely at the expense of the

10 gauge, now used almost entirely for long-range game shooting at large birds. Competitive events for the 10 gauge are almost unheard of.

Since the advent of smokeless powder there has been a trend toward smaller gauges and somewhat lighter guns. Prophecies that the 20 gauge would take over from the 12 gauge, however, have proved untrue. While it *is* much more popular each year, it is not the standard.

The 16-gauge shotgun is a favorite on the continent even as it loses popularity in America because its loads are overlapped by the 20-gauge magnum. In England the 12 gauge holds its rank for very practical reasons: its users are often highly critical of the 20 as a game gun. The .410 and the .28-gauge, both old in service, are largely supported in America by the requirements of skeet.

Major skeet tournaments are fired with four gauges, .410 (really a caliber), 28, 20, and 12, a situation which seems likely to continue despite the complaints of shooters who must buy four guns, four kinds of ammunition, and probably four loading

tools. Trapshooters in America and all international target competitors deal only with the 12 gauge.

In America the 16 gauge has been more popular in the South than in the North and is a remarkably efficient cartridge, accepting 1¼ ounces of shot, the standard 12-gauge "express" load. In practice, it tends to pattern better than the three-inch 20-gauge magnum shell with the same amount of shot, because the 20 must stack the shot in a longer case that encourages deformation.

American makers of repeaters discouraged 16-gauge buyers because some of their 16-gauge guns retain almost the same weight and bulk as the 12 gauge, and the 20 is handicapped to some extent for the same reason. The buyer of a small gauge wants his gun to be lighter and handier. While American builders concentrated on heavier loads for the small gauges, the British went to lighter loads for the 12 gauge, and when it comes to patterning the British have an edge, in principle at least.

A 12 gauge weighing little more than six pounds is not available from American compa-

nies, partly because the trend is toward heavy loads, perhaps as much as 1½ ounces of shot for the "short magnum" that fits the standard 12-gauge chamber. In Britain the load is likely to be even less than America's standard "field load" of 1⅛ ounces of shot. The 20-gauge with three-inch chambers throws a much heavier charge of shot than the ultralight British 12-gauge gun, which may have a shorter chamber than is available in America.

So the American 20 gauge, made either in American or foreign factories, is likely to be heavier than the British 12 gauge. The larger bore consistently throws the more even pattern and produces a shorter string of shot in the air. And the argument over light 12 versus heavy 20 also comes to a seldom mentioned marksmanship factor—bulk.

A virtue of the small gauge is supposed to be its light weight and its "convenient" size, which is not always a help to marksmanship. Since shotguns are mounted quickly in most game shooting, it is desirable for the stock, shoulder, and cheek to fit exactly the same for shot after shot. In trying a new gun a shooter may be impressed by a small stock and frame, ignoring the fact that a small gun can be mounted in a variety of ways. A bulkier stock is more insistent on taking the same position for repeated shots. So bulk, completely aside from any consideration of weight, can be a help or hindrance, depending on the build of the shooter. Even the standard measurements for stock fit will not reveal these vagaries of gun form and many a shooter cannot tell why, for him, one gun shoots better than another.

When the matter of the shot string is considered, the old methods of patterning shotguns by firing them at a metal plate or paper target at a measured distance is not a true indication of how or whether the shot will reach a fast-moving object. Instead of being projected as a flat pattern, or even as a round cluster, the shot actually goes in an extended string and the small bore with its elongated chamber will make for a long procession at target distance. Proponents of the short shot string rightly state that game can be struck by more shot as it goes at an angle to the shooter. Those who prefer an extended string can prove that insufficient lead may sometimes be offset by the lagging shot. There can be no winner to the argument, for it is a matter of how long the range is and how much shot is needed for a kill.

It is in America that "magnum" shotgun loads are most popular, and waterfowl hunters of recent years have frequently gone to the three-inch, 12-gauge magnum throwing 1⅞ ounces of shot, or the "standard" magnum with 1½ ounces. Some hunters have used the 10 gauge with even more pellets. Conservationists, always concerned with shooters who cripple game by shooting at too long a range, know that magnum loads are often used in efforts at increasing range rather than in making cleaner kills at practical distances.

Magnum shotgun loads actually start their shot somewhat slower than most regular shells, simply because the added powder must be slow burning in order to avoid high chamber pressures. Round pellets, however, are so inefficient in their

shape that the slowest and the fastest charges generally have inconsequential velocity differences out where the target is struck.

When shotmakers found many years ago that they were dealing with an impossible variety of shot sizes, they standardized to such an extent that the sizes offered by all of the ammunition companies are now virtually the same. In the ubiquitous 12 gauge the loads include almost anything a shooter could want. In other gauges, such as the 20, there is less choice. For example, a 12-gauge load of 1¼ ounces of Number 8 shot is available for use in open guns on small birds such as quail. On the other hand, the three-inch magnum twenty, which also carries 1¼ ounces of shot, can be had in nothing smaller than Number 7½—enough larger to cause a sparser pattern. It is such differences—plus the fact that arms companies must be guided by demand, whether the public chooses wisely or not—that have led to increased handloading by serious gunners.

It is in choice of shot sizes that many shotgun users disagree, their opinions still sometimes bordering on superstition many years after controlled experiments by manufacturers have provided conclusive evidence. For instance, the choice of shot sizes for waterfowl is still a subject of debate.

Despite thousands of rounds fired in tests showing that large shot penetrate better, there is a small cult of shooters insisting that small shot such as Number 7½ penetrates more efficiently because it can slip between feathers. Of course, there must be sufficient pattern density to strike the target with enough pellets for a clean kill but, given that,

165

Modern hunter "flags" (opposite)
American pronghorns as early
plainsman did. Whitetail
deer hunter uses elaborate
tree stand (left) and elk
hunter uses call (opposite) to
draw rutting bull's attention.
Bull elk (below) loses some caution
during rut, when seeking females.

the large shot is undeniably better. The issue is confused by range and by the tightness of the pattern.

In the matter of turkey hunting, experts tend toward smaller shot for completely different reasons. Turkey hunting, a renewed sport that is more popular than ever after half a century in which the bird struggled back from near-oblivion, attracts some of the best-qualified woodsmen in America.

The turkey hunter is one of the proudest clans of all, studying turkey language with hundreds of different types of mechanical calls and engaging in endless ruses of concealment. His gun may have its every gleaming part covered by camouflage tape, and he has learned to become one with the forest and its residents, unnoticed by squirrels or raccoons only a few feet away. His patience is unending. The turkey is often called big game, although most turkey hunting is done with shotguns.

Many of the best turkey hunters insist that since it is very difficult to kill a turkey with any sort of body shot, the proper size shot is Number 7½, aimed at the head and neck. There are others who say Number 2 shot will penetrate the body sufficiently; the argument is endless. Since most turkeys are shot on the ground, requiring that the shotgun be aimed somewhat like a rifle, the aiming spot can be chosen. Perhaps the most common shot size is around 4 or 5 for the ground shot, the second shell holding larger shot for a flying or wounded bird. Rob Keck, turkey-calling champion and constant experimenter in his favorite game, chooses 7½ shot and exhibits patterns fired over turkey outlines as proof of its efficiency.

While there are ceaseless disagreements about shotgun and rifle choices for various kinds of hunting, there is at least one sport in which the argument crosses the line between shotguns and rifles: the hunting of whitetail deer in eastern United States. The law, of course, dictates the choice in some populated areas where rifles are prohibited and shotguns must be used, whether with single slugs or with buckshot.

Still, in the dull and changing light deep in swamps and forests, where the hunter waits in silence and listens for the rise and fall of the deer hound's song, there is ever a question: rifle or shotgun? There are some very brushy areas in the South where hounds are nearly a necessity to move enough deer to give hunters any chances at all, and there are many parts of the United States where the use of dogs would be an unfair advantage. In most deer

167

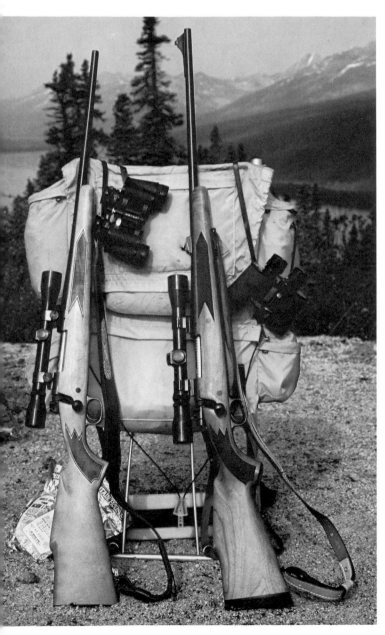

Telescopic sights and fine binoculars (below) are important for mountain big-game hunt. Sheep hunters (right) climb with white camouflage in snow country. Dall ram (far right) is most northern of American wild sheep. Packers lash down caribou (opposite, bottom) antlers in wilderness big-game camp.

habitat the use of dogs is illegal.

It is in the use of hounds that the shotgun is especially helpful, for the whitetail is likely to be a briefly sighted shadow and the hunter must often shoot while it is moving swiftly at close range with the added obligation of positive identification. Even in these conditions there are those who prefer rifles, preferably fast-firing ones.

The whitetail deer is the most plentiful of America's big game, ranging from the great four-hundred-pound specimens in the Northeast to adult bucks that weigh less than a fourth of that in the Southwest and Florida. Some of the most popular deer rifles, such as Winchester, Savage, and Marlin lever actions, have changed little in more than seventy-five years. They have been intended for fast operation at close-to-moderate range and their cartridges are much the same as those introduced with the guns themselves.

Semiautomatics, greatly improved in recent years, have a large share of the market and a few pump rifles are used, the favorites of those raised with pump shotguns. Bolt-action rifles have been slow to invade the brush, becoming more popular only as the telescopic sight was accepted for close-range shooting.

The shotgun hunter for deer has been a critical customer of guns because the performance of a given barrel with buckshot has always been unpredictable. Thus some ancient guns with battered stocks and the pitting of fifty years of intermittent rust have been treasured because with a given size of buckshot they produce a deadly pattern at a prac-

*Precise marksmanship in game
country is aided by a dead
rest and shooter (right)
uses a bit of padding to
keep rifle from recoiling
away from log. Grizzly bear
(below) and larger brown
are the only truly dangerous
American game. They will
attack unprovoked, and if
provoked can prove deadly
to unwary hunter.*

tical range. Like the competitive clay-target shooter, the shotgunning deer hunter actually tests his gun. To him the choke marking on the barrel must be proved—with buckshot.

Through the years there have been innumerable efforts at making buckshot stay together better during its flight, usually a matter of packing some sort of granulated filler material around the shot inside the shell case. In recent years there has been great improvement in packing materials, and performance has improved. Whereas a pattern of smaller shot may be reasonably efficient on small game, even with the loss of a few deformed pellets, a buckshot load of a dozen pellets becomes a tricky package. The three-inch magnum 12 gauge has increased in popularity as a deer gun. Most authorities consider the 16-gauge minimal for buckshot on deer.

The rifled slug, a heavy, slow-moving missile that will work in a shotgun, regardless of choke, has been produced for a long time in both Europe and America. It is a much more efficient descendant of the round ball that for centuries went through the smoothbore musket.

The rifled slug is a short-range "bullet" of great weight, and while the rifling in the slug itself probably causes minimal rotation, the improved accuracy over the round ball (hardly ever used in modern shotguns) is mainly due to its balance. The best known of the slugs is the German Brenneke, little changed since its introduction in 1898.

In areas where the rifle is prohibited by law because of dense population and level ground, some hunters have taken pains to develop smooth-bore combinations to extend slug ranges beyond the fifty or sixty yards that is nearly the outside limit of the average shooter and typical shotgun. Most of the large American shotgun builders have introduced cylinder-bored, short-barreled slug guns, built on the standard repeater actions with adjustable sights, and some low-powered telescopes have been used.

There have been guns with shallow rifling at the muzzle, similar to the "Paradox" of long ago, and there have been tests with shallow full-length rifling, although such guns are not legal in "shotgun" areas. But while many riflemen scorn any big-game use of the shotgun there is terrain where the advantage of one over the other is debatable and other terrain where the shotgun is supreme.

Even as Europeans, especially the English, engage in continuous discussion of the double shotgun versus the American repeater and the over-under versus the side-by-side, American riflemen disagree among themselves, often violently, over the merits of bullet weight versus muzzle velocity and the closely allied "magnum" issue. Magnum cartridges, generally speaking, are simply large-capacity cases driving bullets of the same diameter and weights as "standard" cartridges of less velocity.

Because of some misunderstanding, and possibly because of a little deliberate deception, there have been pitched verbal battles concerning many calibers, both wildcat and commercial. When the large ammunition companies began to encourage handloading after World War II (following a long period during which they felt the handloader was a competitor), American riflemen delved into technical

ballistics further than ever before. Literally thousands of experimental cartridges were loaded, many of them to be adopted as commercial rounds and many others to be abandoned, not necessarily because they were poor performers but because they were near duplicates of accepted cartridges.

The words "overbore capacity" became common among students of ballistics. This meant simply that an overbore-capacity cartridge case would contain more powder than could be efficiently burned within the barrel while the bullet was on its way to the muzzle. And here powder selection and barrel length became more important than was at first apparent.

One of the unusually frustrating matters for the student of loads was the chronographing of factory ammunition, which was usually done with a rather long barrel, capable of economical use of the powder. Then when a custom rifle was built with a much shorter barrel, the extra speed the shooter sought dissolved in recoil and the muzzle flash of unburned powder. To the amusement of chronographers, such shooters often paid extra for more recoil and noise and hardly any added velocity at all. This folly was largely American, European shooters showing more moderation.

The typical mountain or plains hunting rifle of 1950 had a 24- or 22-inch barrel with the shorter one preferred by most shooters. Most magnum cartridges as typified by the Weatherby line of ammunition required 24 inches of barrel to produce their startling ballistics and 26 inches was better.

Of course, the velocity debate was no

longer one of "punkin rollers" against "fast" thirty-thirties. It raged about choices between the remarkably efficient .30-06 and the 300 H. & H. or between the .270 and the milder 7 × 57, or between the .270 and the swifter 270 Weatherby Magnum, or between the 7 × 61 Sharpe and Hart and the 7mm Remington Magnum.

The question with medium-sized game was one of diminishing returns and just how much advantage was gained by two hundred feet more per second out where the bullet struck. The cost might be considerably more rifle weight and a longer barrel. Perhaps the best illustration came with two very old cartridges—the .30-06 and the 300 Holland and Holland, both of which were excellent in bolt-action rifles. The English Holland and Holland firm introduced their cartridge in 1920 as a "super 30." In the thirties American manufacturers began to build rifles for it and the American version of the cartridge was somewhat faster.

There was no doubt that the .300 had advantages as a long-range target load and it was very popular in Africa, as well as for America's heavier animals. However, its larger case demanded a longer barrel than the .30-06 for efficiency, and its detractors said the extra velocity was too slight for the cost in recoil, noise, extra weight, and barrel length.

In fact, the listed velocity for the .300 shows slightly more than two hundred feet per second more than the .30-06 with similar bullets, a matter of about one fourteenth more speed, so the disagreement can never be resolved on the basis of how

Looking is a great part of big-game hunting, especially in mountain country. Hunter (left) is equipped with pack frame and good binoculars. Good equipment can provide the added help that allows the big-game hunter more than the usual trophies.

much difference that amount would make on impact.

Then came the more powerful thirties, most of them beginning with a blown-out form of the 300 H. & H. and with considerably more velocity. The 300 Weatherby became leader of the contingent of high-speed .30-caliber rifles with some two hundred f.p.s. more than the 300 H. & H. Others of the best-known "big thirties" included the 308 Norma Magnum from Sweden and the 300 Winchester Magnum, the latter becoming a leader because of its association with probably the most famous firearms concern in the world. The ballistics are similar in all of the big thirties.

By the 1950s the .270 was considered a mild cartridge, indeed, but its 130-grain bullet at well beyond three thousand f.p.s. had proven a superb killer for deer and antelope-sized game. It was never widely accepted in Europe until American demands caused European rifles to be built for it.

Of course, the difference between big and slower bullets and small and faster bullets on game is a matter of how the hit is made. Heavy bullets are known for penetration; light ones at high speed have a nearly explosive effect. So an elk-sized animal struck in the lungs with a .270 at high speed might receive tremendous internal damage. Struck by a .375 or a .338 with harder bullets at slower speed the animal might not be killed so quickly; still, if the bullet must pass through heavy muscle and bone the heavier one has an advantage.

Shooters prove fickle and some cartridges and rifles that proved highly successful show results hardly discernible from those that have almost disappeared. There were a number of 7mm cartridges of very similar ballistics. The 7mm Remington, a magnum load with a belted case, is now their leader with many factory rifles built for it. The 7mm Sharpe and Hart (introduced with a Shultz and Larsen rifle built expressly for it) is much less popular, though at one time it received glowing publicity, and the 7mm Weatherby Magnum remains popular. There has been a trend toward short cases with large capacity for use in actions of moderate length. All of these are truly high-velocity loads, adequate for all North American big game, although rated as minimal for the great bears by some authorities.

The most controversial smallbore rifle had been the 220 Swift, introduced by Winchester in 1935 and driving a 45-grain bullet at more than four thousand f.p.s. With a full powder charge, it was a devastating performer on varmints. The cartridge fell into disfavor because of fast barrel erosion, only to revive with better barrels and something less than its heaviest charges. Winchester discontinued rifles for it in 1964.

The 264 Winchester Magnum began with good press as an extremely fast load for medium game, then acquired a bad reputation for short barrel life in some quarters. Few rifles are now built for it.

Shooters glory in variety and argue incessantly about the merits of certain guns and systems, sometimes in the face of indisputable performance figures. Their allegiances make hunting, target shooting, gun collecting, and gun debate a variety of hobbies within the broad confines of sporting guns of the world.

8

Precision and Perfection

In the twentieth century man runs faster, jumps higher, and lifts more than he ever has before. He also shoots straighter, and although this is due in part to modern technology which produces the superior guns he fires, his control over flesh and blood and rebelling nerves has reached a level never before accomplished. Twentieth century man has more power than ever.

Lying on a shooting mat is a young woman, part of a long line of shooters that make a hodgepodge of colors and glistening equipment. She draws herself into a prison of concentration and shuts out the rumbling sounds of traffic and murmurs of conversation in the background, sounds that barely penetrate her mufflike ear protectors.

She moves deliberately as she arranges her gear and notes her pulse seems moderate; she had already covertly examined her hand to see if it quivered unduly. Her heavy leather coat, properly adjusted, seems to offer steadying support as it was intended to with no disturbing strain anywhere, and her floppy hat helps to shut out the rest of the world. Her own special universe consists of a few yards of delicate mirage over cropped grass, a coal-black bullseye magnified in the big scope, and the sharply etched crosshairs that cut it in four equal segments.

There is the little wind gauge with its busy mill producing a dainty whir, her personal wind gauge, and there is her own timer, visible without moving her head, despite the blinders at the sides of her shooting eyeglasses. There is the block of .22 long rifle cartridges, carefully counted out. Made with meticulous care on the other side of the Atlantic, those special cartridges had been shipped past millions of other .22 cartridges in hundreds of stores across America, chosen for today because in her gun they have had the shade of extra accuracy that wins smallbore matches.

A small, high cloud moves its shadow across the range and for a moment she wonders if her amber glasses would have been better, but it is soon gone. She assesses her position once more, feeling solid with the earth and the thin shooting mat and with the sling's arm cuff snugly steadying the heavy rifle with its big barrel. The broad fore end rests on her gloved hand and the crosshairs hang steady as she feels the serrated trigger with a finger that tightens ever so slightly, a human mechanism almost a part of the rifle. And she wishes the shot more than consciously pulling the trigger to feel a gentle tremor in the big stock and hearing the petulant spitting sound from the muzzle as other spitting reports sound up and down the line, shut out from her universe. She slides back the bolt, slick and precise in its extraction and ejection, and then loads another cartridge to fire again before the wind changes, and then she checks her spotting scope on its goosenecked stand at her left. Her contest is more with her nervous system than with the long line of shooters, each with his own contest.

The competitive rifleman is a scientist, a psychologist with himself as a patient, and he deals with a culmination of the gun-building craft, one branch of firearm development whose precision is more in evidence on a rectangle of paper than in its own appearance.

The smallbore target rifle seldom has inlays, engraving, or even a highly figured stock. However expensive or however lovingly it is built it is a tool, pure and simple. The .22 smallbore rifle is fired in several kinds of matches, the outdoor prone match being one of the more demanding, despite the fact that it seems simple, for the shooting is precise and the equipment must be right.

Competition has been the developer of rifle and ammunition accuracy, from the indoor smallbore match to the big-bore effort at a thousand yards. Supreme accuracy on the range has come from better barrel construction and rifling, better breech closures, extremely fine trigger letoffs, precise telescopic and aperture sights, and the careful balancing of powder and bullets.

In every form of rifle or shotgun competition there has been a predictable sequence of development. Invariably, the competition starts as a means of measuring ability at game shooting. In every case the ability of the competitors soon surpasses the capabilities of the guns used, so guns are then improved. When the guns become good enough for perfect or nearly perfect scores it is necessary to change the course of fire or the targets so there will be fewer ties.

Invariably the development of guns used has been toward specialization and away from the practical hunting arm. Of all the officially recognized competitive shooting sports in the world today, only a very few employ guns that would be practical for hunting. The pressure has always been toward alterations that, in total, produce specialized target arms.

There are some near exceptions. In skeet the stock measurements are usually the same as for hunting and the barrels are satisfactorily bored for close-range field shooting. But skeet guns tend to be somewhat heavier than the ideal in field guns. The new sport of shooting at metal silhouette targets with rifles and pistols began with practical hunting arms but almost immediately there appeared custom "silhouette" rifles, slightly awkward for a hunting trip and straining the "hunting-rifle" specifications.

But as racing cars have contributed to design of the family sedan, so has competition contributed to the factory hunting rifle or shotgun. And the highly developed sport of formal target shooting needs no excuse for specialized guns. In most cases the user of a bulky international "free rifle" has put more into his sport than any weekend deer hunter, and perhaps he has no interest at all in hunting.

Even in the early nineteenth century there were competitions between makers of accurate barrels in which the guns were placed on solid rests so that the human element of aiming would be minimized as much as possible. It was more than a hundred years before that sport developed strongly and somewhere along the line it acquired the name of "benchrest shooting." Beginning with the long-range matches shortly after the Civil War there has been an unbroken series of big-bore competitions with military rifles or their close relatives. Such shooting has been sponsored by the military of many countries and some of that competition has always been restricted to military rifles.

177

The Schuetzen rifles of Germany were used for target shooting before they became popular in America and were visible forerunners of the modern international rifles used in the Olympic matches and other events of the International Shooting Union. It may be that the German and Austrian Schuetzen was developed from the jaeger rifle, but it had a distinctive silhouette and was intended for deliberate offhand firing. The stock was heavy with graceful sweeps of design and carried an elaborate cheekpiece. The buttplate was deeply hooked, with a long toe to aid in the rifle's balance. There were double-set triggers and usually an intricate finger lever to operate the falling-block type of action. The elaborate peep sights were generally mounted on the tang (behind the breech). In most forms of Schuetzen competition there were palm rests extended below the fore end so that the left elbow (for a right-handed shooter) could be rested on the hip.

The targets originated in Europe and were used also in America, and had a great number of scoring rings. There was a variety of calibers, the most popular in the most highly developed form of Schuetzen competition being the 8.15 × 46R cartridge of about 1893, using a lead bullet. The competitors were generally handloaders. The form of shooting was adopted by numerous clubs in America with a variety of cartridges and virtually disappeared with World War I, when anything associated with Germany became unpopular there. It was time for development of American forms of target shooting.

The Schuetzen type of rifle was the vehicle for the famous barrelmakers of America. George Schoyen, H. M. Pope, and A. O. Zischang were perhaps the best known of the early twentieth century. A. W. Peterson, associated for a time with Schoyen in Denver, also made contributions in all phases of rifle building and telescopic-sight construction. Some of the Schuetzen rifles were built in .22 caliber, although the more dramatic performances came from larger bores.

Fired from a bench, some of the old target barrels, laboriously made with relatively simple machinery, produced incredible groups. Charles W. Rowland, a famous benchrest shooter, fired ten shots into a group measuring .725 inch at two-hundred yards, using a .32-40 Pope rifle. Shooting offhand at two-hundred yards, a Schuetzen master named W. A. Kuntz is said to have hit a silver dollar five times straight with a 14½-pound Schoyen Ballard rifle. In some matches of the early twentieth century, the heavy target rifles were used from the standing position with long balance weights extending back over the shooter's shoulder.

Although the Schuetzen rifles had much the same conformation as the modern free rifle, there was generally more attention to artistic stock structure, checkering, and figured wood. The free rifle is more utilitarian in appearance.

There were many years during which the qualifications of the breechloader were in doubt concerning target accuracy. Some of the best rifles were loaded with false muzzles that enabled the shooter to start his bullet evenly into the rifling. It was an accurate combination of breechloaded powder, case and primer, and muzzleloader bullets.

Complete Perazzi skeet set (opposite) consists of single stock and action with four barrel sets for various events. Italian Perazzi has become leader in American and international tourneys. Skeet shooter (left) uses top form with autoloading shotgun, preferred by many for reduced recoil.

After World War I the bolt action began to take over all forms of target shooting, and as America began its own form of smallbore tournament, the Winchester Model 52 target rifle was introduced in 1920 for the .22 long rifle cartridge. The .22 long began to fade although the .22 short remained as a plinking cartridge and was later to be used for Olympic rapid-fire pistol shooting at short range. The "long" had been simply the long rifle case with the "short's" light bullet.

Other American companies built smallbore target rifles and for years it was believed almost any of them would shoot better than the shooter could hold and aim but, as is invariably the case, human efficiency began to demand better equipment. Shooting skill has continually outdistanced the gun.

The changes were in lock time, in trigger letoff, in barrel accuracy—and then in ammunition. American match ammunition for the twenty-two was somewhat more expensive than "standard" cartridges and was more precisely built, but American companies rested too long on their laurels and eventually the British Eley ammunition virtually took over in serious smallbore competition. Then in the 1970s the Americans tried harder and the market was in the balance.

Indoor or "gallery" smallbore shooting has been a major influence in the advancement of marksmanship, especially in schools and colleges. A large share of the winning competitive shooters on the national and international scene began with position shooting (standing, kneeling, sitting, and prone) indoors, and some of the best have represented military teams after they left school.

In international competition there is shooting at fifty meters with the twenty-two and at three hundred meters with centerfire cartridges with the 308 Winchester, the most popular for those courses of fire. For nearly a hundred years the .30-caliber bullets have led in long-range competitive shooting, regardless of the size or shape of the cartridge.

Neither of the free rifles is a hunting arm. They are built for precise aiming rather than for climbing mountains or crossing swamps. The shooter has developed his own uniform for the task: he wears a leather jacket that can be adjusted to give body support wherever needed and even his boots are made to steady his frame in the stylized positions proven most efficient.

The various forms of American high-power target shooting are more practical for the hunter or the soldier, some forms requiring truly rapid fire with reloading and position acquirement included in the actual firing time. Although the rifles used in both iron-sight and scope-sight competitions are quite heavy for most hunting, the hunter would feel at home with them.

Thirty caliber and 7mm rifles are most popular in the really long-range events which allow "any rifle." Bolt actions, usually customized, are the winners at one thousand yards and such cartridges as the 300 Winchester (similar to the 300 Weatherby) are employed in heavy prone rifles with high-powered scopes in some matches. The 300 H. & H. has

been largely replaced at one thousand yards, although it was once the most regular winner.

Such powerful rifles would not be necessary for long-range accuracy if it were not for the vagaries of wind, but the best way of combating wind is to fire a long, heavy bullet at high speed. Most of the one-thousand-yard bullets are close to 200 grains, a weight used for grizzly bears.

The influence of service firearms cannot be ignored for the military cartridges have not only served in military rifle matches but have had enormous influence on all big-game hunting equipment. The development of service rifles has taken strange turns—not always for more accuracy, power, or convenience but directly in keeping with military philosophy. That philosophy has changed repeatedly.

When the .30-40 Krag cartridge replaced such heavy loads as the .45-70 it was a move toward higher velocity, and when the .30-06 appeared to fight two widely spaced European and Asian wars for the United States it was chosen for superior power and accuracy. The bolt action was replaced in World War II by a semiautomatic rifle (the Garand) but the same cartridge was retained.

When the NATO countries adopted the 7.62 cartridge (308 Winchester in civilian caliber) as their standard military round they made a slight backward move in velocity but the new cartridge, which proved excellent for hunting and target shooting, was small enough to use the advantage of a short action. The American military rifle, with the M-14 chambered for it, the 7.62 could be fired at full automatic, illegal for civilian use, but a wide variety of

hunting rifles in all action forms were highly successful.

And then the military chose a new direction entirely. The trend had been toward firepower and "saturation" fire and marksmanship training had been reduced to a minimum in most of the armed forces. Now, after a century of powerful cartridges, the United States adopted a small, light rifle that used the 5.56mm cartridge (223 Remington in civilian form). It was an entirely new concept and the military cartridge had become a "varmint" load instead of a "big-game" load.

Although the .223 was accurate at short distances it could not compete with the older loads over the extended target ranges. The M-16 rifle made for it could fire automatically when desired, most of those who carried it had little or no marksmanship training, and to the despair of believers in military riflery the little gun went to Vietnam and the tiny bullets were sprayed in a way that that expended more cartridges per enemy casualty than in any other war. So civilian rifles were used for some sniping, and the big-game hunter turned abruptly away from the military.

Probably the greatest shooting game of all for the hunting rifleman is the new silhouette matches which originated in Mexico and are intended for the high-powered hunting rifle. It may be said to be a carry-over from the shooting gallery where customers pay for shots at little metal cutouts of animals, boats, and other things, using .22 shorts.

But it is an outdoor game and in order to score, the shooter must knock over the metal cut-

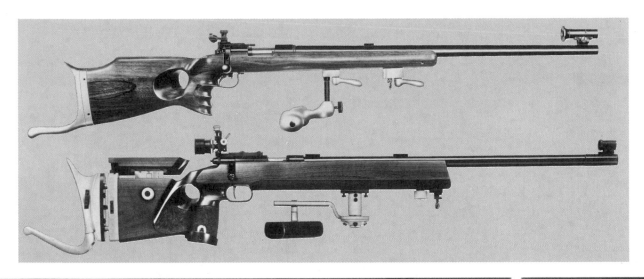

out. Since the longest range is five hundred meters and the target is heavy, he must use a big-game cartridge. Even the 6mm loads of the 243 Winchester and the 6mm Remington are too light. The most popular cartridge is the .308, and in the early years of the competition the rules have held shooters to hunting rifles that could actually be carried in the field. Telescopic sights are used.

Strangest of all in the silhouette game's appeal is that the course is so difficult that all the scores are low, a match being won with less than half of the targets knocked over. In the past the chief complaint of target shooting, both rifle and shotgun, has been the prevalence of scores that were too high, occasioning many ties and extended shooting. So far, the silhouette course has been kept too difficult for that and it is excellent training for big-game hunting.

If the new silhouette shooting has a competitor in the business of hunting training it is the international running bore matches in which the shooter fires at moving targets. So far the rifles for it have been more specialized than the hunting arms applied to the steel silhouettes.

In 1955 a big-game rifle that could group within three inches at one hundred yards was considered quite satisfactory. Four inches was considered practical for a woods rifle and the rare factory model that could make a "minute of angle" group (about one inch across at one hundred yards) was treasured. Twenty years later there had been more improvement in factory accuracy than had occurred in the past sixty years and the one-inch group from the factory rifle was quite common.

The reasons were better inletting (the fitting of metal to stock wood), better sealing of the stock (so that it would not warp), better barrels, faster lock time, and much better bullets. Later bullets were so well balanced that their high-speed spinning in flight did not carry them off course. It took a while to realize the importance of this; once fully recognized the improvements came rapidly.

The development of better factory rifles, calibers, and ammunition came largely from a little-known branch of target shooting, the benchrest experts. In benchrest shooting the competitor must be a good shot and must have a thorough understanding of ballistics but may be even more of a technician than the target shooter who supports his rifle with his hands and body. It is benchrest shooters who have been responsible for development of most of the most recent cartridges.

Their rifles range from some that would be quite practical on Pennsylvania woodchucks or Idaho marmots to those that are more complex in construction than artillery of a few years back, and are much more controllable. Most practical benchrest rifles from the hunter's standpoint are those in varmint and sporter classes. The sporting-rifle class has an upper limit of ten and a half pounds and must be larger than .22 caliber; the light varmint class with the same weight limit uses .22-caliber ammunition.

Benchrest riflemen have been leaders in systems of bedding or fitting actions to stocks. The slightest undue pressure by wood against metal can destroy hairsplitting accuracy, and fiberglass is inherently productive of the most stable stocks. Ex-

tremely short but heavy barrels have been used in order to gain stiffness, for much inaccuracy has been caused by barrel whip or vibration. Most winning rifles are custom affairs. The shape of the action is important for the best bedding, with a flat-bottomed action preferred.

The 222 Remington, a mild-mannered little varmint cartridge introduced in 1950, is the basis for most of the best benchrest rifles and has bullet speeds slightly below the 223 Remington or the 222 Remington Magnum, which duplicate the velocities of the military 223.

Winning groups at one hundred yards run under one-quarter inch and appear as one ragged hole. In benchrest competition, location of the group on the target does not affect the score.

The perfectly balanced bullet will spin without wobble on the way to the target and its inherent accuracy is involved with combinations of length, diameter, and total weight as well as its shape. Even if the bullet is perfectly designed for its single trip from muzzle to target, it must be mated to the chamber and barrel that fire it, and barrel and chamber diameters are critical since there is some variation even in a single caliber. Barrel life is limited so the master shooter keeps careful count of the number of shots fired, ever wary of the slightest accuracy loss through bore wear.

Benchrest ammunition is almost invariably assembled by the shooter himself, and within a given caliber there is a wide variety of powder charges. A particular rifle, bullet, and cartridge case will be most accurate with a certain weight of powder of a certain make and with a particular brand of primer. Shooters may prefer cases coming from a particular factory run. It is an endless quest for uniformity in all components.

As a successor to the falling-block type of action, the bolt has been supreme in all sorts of target shooting and is widely regarded as the most accurate of hunting rifles. However, there have been commercial semiautomatics, pumps, and lever actions which show more accuracy than do some standard commercial bolt actions. This does not mean that they have benchrest potential but as hunting rifles they are acceptably accurate.

And the semiautomatic target pistol as fired with one hand has virtually taken over in all but the "free pistol" matches. The free pistol is a tool of international competition and has little relation to hunting pistols.

The varmint shooters, once charmed by the explosive effects of extreme velocity, have been inclined toward finer accuracy, often obtained with more modest bullet speeds. In recent years some of the more powerful varmint cartridges have been adopted as combination rounds, useful for deer-sized game. The .25-06, the .30-06 cartridge necked down to .25 caliber, has proved a superb long-range varminter and is now fired in unaltered factory rifles after long tenure as a wildcat. It is popular as a deer and pronghorn load as well.

The 243 Winchester and 6mm Remington, begun as heavy-duty varmint cartridges, have excellent records on deer-sized game. As a pure varminter, the .22-250, an adaptation of the old Savage

*The single-barrel Ithaca
trap gun in 20 gauge (below,
left) with fine Parker trap
model (below, right) is
unusual. Most trap guns are
12's. Opposite, breech
sections (below) with American
engraving. Franz Sodia over-
under set (opposite, above)
in hard case has barrels
for all gauges of skeet
competition plus trap
boring and carved wood.*

.250-3000 deer cartridge, has become a factory load after prominence as a wildcat. Smallest of the newer factory varmint cartridges is the 17 Remington. The most flattering statement about factory rifles and ammunition today is that they are again approaching human capabilities, whether afield or on the range.

None of the current target events is a spectator sport but the watcher of a modern skeet tournament can find subtle events within it that explain why the bane of skeet has been perfect scores. The skeet champion on Station 3, where his shots will be at nearly a right angle, addresses the center post with his muzzle, briskly swings it then toward the low house, which will give him a shot going from right to left, and calls for his target.

With the clack of the trap, unseen within the house, the disk flashes across the field and the shooter's concentration closes out all else as his gun quickly traces the familiar groove as it has done so many thousands of times. And at the point where it has happened so many thousands of times, just before the center peg, the target breaks, a haze of pieces wobbling off toward the ground.

But the shooter's face, to that point a mask of concentration on each shot, shows a flicker of apprehension, instantly concealed. As he awaits his turn for the next left angle his expression is calculating and thoughtful, for the large piece of target had come from the back of the whirling clay and he knows his pattern was too far ahead. Hits that are not fully centered can mean some trend from his set routine, a trend that might soon mean a miss on a left-angle target.

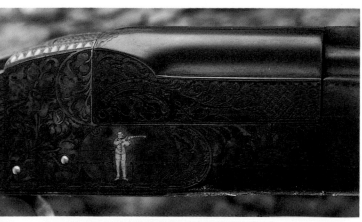

On Station 4 his shot appears the same as usual but there is a large piece from the broken target again, this time from the front. The pattern is a bit behind and he knows he has overcompensated. Then, like an artilleryman who deals with a straddled target, he waits for his low target from Station 5, and this time it disappears in a puff of smoked pitch.

The shooter is back in his groove again, having dealt with a problem in precision that the casual shooter would neither recognize nor deal with, and he shoots with routine concentration, the difference between the champion and the ordinary shooter. All skeet shooters can break all targets but they deal with human frailties of concentration, nervous control, and muscular coordination.

The occasional weekend skeet shooter tries for 23 of 25 or 25 straight but the champion works toward the hundreds without a miss. A few years ago a skeet tournament ended in a tie, two shooters having fired themselves into near exhaustion with the 12 gauge without missing, while the tired judges began to doubt their ability to call a chipped target.

Like most shooting games skeet began as training for hunting—in this case close-range shotgunning—the name "skeet" coming from a Scandinavian word for "shoot" in a naming contest in 1925. The skeet field with its two traps in high and low houses was adapted from a form in which the shooters walked a complete circle. A half-circle was obviously easier to handle and required much less room. Spectators and clubhouses could be close to a half circle with safety. Very shortly skeet became an end in itself and open-bored shotguns were being built especially for it. Eventually there were events for the four gauges used today.

Field shooters seeking practice on skeet fields soon found there were several "trick" shots requiring expertise in "groove" shooting, in which the target takes a difficult but established route that can be memorized. For one thing, the doubles consisted of one target going away and one incomer, hardly common in upland gunning. For another there were some unusual incomers to be hit at close range from Station 8 in the center of the field, a shot seldom used in hunting. But these shots were not difficult for the experienced skeet shooter, for it is a game of established patterns, and today's targets, unless there are severe winds, will go about as yesterday's did.

At first the gun was held low when the targets were called for, and then in a departure from hunting conditions the shooter was allowed to mount his gun before calling for a target. This produced such long runs of hits that the larger and more efficient guns were scored in the missless hundreds and officials of the National Skeet Shooting Association sought a means of lowering the scores. They settled on faster targets but the masters adapted to those quickly and there undoubtedly will be other changes.

Trapshooting had changed little since clay pigeons were first fired at from five different stations with their exact direction unknown to the shooter. While the skeet guns stayed close to hunting dimensions, the trap gun became long, heavy, and straight-stocked to allow for an invariably rising target and the shorter angles.

Trapshooting, with more participants than skeet, is operated with a handicapping system in which less proficient shooters fire from a closer range. It too has suffered from too many perfect scores and resultant shootoffs that have found tired gunners working on the ragged edge of their nerves, sometimes in the tricky light of dusk.

International skeet and international clay-pigeon competitions came along to reduce the likelihood of long runs and ties but the Americans were reluctant to accept them and for years their teams were humiliated by shooters who had been trained on more difficult courses of fire. The international games required special equipment and international clay-pigeon installations were almost prohibitively expensive, for they required long trenches with a number of costly traps. Modified fields were set up for practice, however.

International skeet used a very fast target that few American setups could handle without some modification, and the target is fired with the gun below the elbow when the bird is called for. The

easier shots are eliminated with more difficult doubles called for and the "groove" as in American skeet is hard to acquire. For some time American shooters in that sport came largely from military teams. Finally, civilians began to break in.

"Olympic trench" or "international clay pigeon" involves a shooter with a mounted gun and targets that fly at very high speed at wide angles both laterally and vertically. As in live-pigeon shooting the gunner is allowed two shots at each target. Both of the international games require fast reflexes and the top competitors tend to be youthful, even though they may not be able to beat older hands at American skeet and trap.

It is trap and skeet that have brought forth some of the finest shotguns in the world, many beautifully engraved and inlaid, but it is in their utility that they gain the respect of competition shooters, who fire countless thousands of rounds without complaint. At trap, especially, they depart widely from hunting guns and the art of barrel choking reaches its peak in the attainment of given pattern percentages with certain ammunition, critically judged by handicap shooters who may stand anywhere from sixteen yards to twenty-seven yards from the trap.

It is trap that has brought the "release trigger," a trigger that fires when the finger is relaxed rather than when it pulls. The mechanism was developed to aid those who tended to flinch with the trigger pull. The shooter pulls the release trigger, calls for his target, and then releases the trigger when he is ready to fire.

The ventilated rib is standard on trap guns and very high ribs have been developed in order to allow a shooter to use an extremely straight stock, and the plane of the barrel is so low that its apparent recoil is reduced.

Although the side-by-side double has virtually disappeared from the trap fields the over-under gains ground constantly, often fitted with a single barrel for use when a second shot is not used at doubles or international clay pigeon. The pump-gun remains a very popular trap gun and the Winchester Model 12 in a trap model was the undisputed leader for many years. Although it is no longer built in a field or skeet model, it is still sold for trapshooting with appropriate stocking. In pumpguns for trap, its chief competitor is the Remington 870, latest of a long line of Remington pumps and especially smooth in action despite a minimum of handwork.

The pump has a balance well suited for American trap but it is nearly matched by some of the very long and heavy barrels appearing on singleshot and over-under guns, a length of up to 32 or even 34 inches being common in recent years.

For those bothered by recoil during long sessions of shooting, the gas-operated automatic is being used a great deal at both skeet and trap, although its ejection of empty shells is a nuisance to reloaders.

While target guns are available at a wide range of prices, their costs average higher than those bought for hunting. Guns have become better, ammunition has become better, and shooters still improve.

9

For the Chosen Few

Aside from guns valued for their part in historical events, there is a quiet traffic in very expensive sporting guns. These acquire great value in several ways. Some are sought by collectors purely because they are scarce; usually these are models made in very small numbers. The ornate guns of centuries ago have been treasured as art objects for many years, especially those of Europe and Asia, some of which were even decorated with precious metals or jewels.

In more recent years there have been guns which combine art and craft, highly efficient arms with such meticulous workmanship that their very mechanisms have become collectors' prizes. They are the work of lifetime makers, often generations of masters who stood at the same benches. Such workmen grew fewer with the rush and demands of modern production, but the gun arts, far from being lost, revived in a new demand for fine arms in the late twentieth century, which brought forth better guns than ever in some types.

When the flintlock fowling piece of Louis XIII of France was bought some years ago by the Metropolitan Museum of Art for $300,000, the sale was reported as that of the world's costliest gun. Its current dollar value in the light of inflation might be a great deal more. The sum seemed less spectacular by 1978, when new British best-grade shotguns with conservative engraving and no precious metals were priced at $25,000.

The world's gun lovers do not seek publicity and it is quite likely that $100,000 for a fine gun of some historical significance is not exceptional. Competitive shooters have repeatedly paid more than the price of a luxury automobile for a skeet gun with extra barrels, and many double rifles or shotguns with some decoration have cost as much as modest suburban homes. Prices of firearms are closely associated with the shooting sports because they reflect the appreciation of fine arms.

The zenith of ornate French firearms was reached about the middle of the seventeenth century, and some of the guns built for royalty were so decorated as to barely retain the outline of firearms. As their shapes were impractical for shooting purposes they were mainly vehicles for decoration; some very similar Asiatic guns did not shoot at all.

The names attached to most fine arms are recognized everywhere. There are a number of such British names and a few from Belgium, Finland, Germany, Austria, Italy, and Spain. But there also are some masterpieces known only to serious students. In these cases only a few guns have been made in a lifetime by a single worker or family of workers, who often lived in a secluded part of the world. Such workers dwelled in northern Italy and near modest shops of the British Isles. A sportsman who knows well the names of Westley-Richards, Merkel, Francotte, or Perazzi may never have heard of these other artists, but their "off-brand" products are eagerly sought at high prices by the few who know and can afford them.

In the late twentieth century few of the old names had disappeared entirely. In the British gun industry, a series of mergers made the situation complex but it was possible to find someone making a few guns bearing nearly any of the famous names. The broker who handled fine guns reported some makes appeared so rarely that ordering them was hardly worthwhile. Even the best-known makes with the largest plants had waiting lists that ran more than two years at a minimum.

The strange situation of an expensive product in demand and yet hard to secure was involved in inflationary currency, the passing of fine handwork in some quarters, and the fact that fine firearms have been good investments for many years. When guns have required considerable handwork, their prices have gone steadily upward, and the supply of some guns has gone steadily downward with the number of workmen capable of producing them.

And there are many gunmakers who have undertaken to overcome a regional reputation for shoddy merchandise. In Spain, where some of the high-grade double guns of the later twentieth century were produced, there have been a great many cheap guns built for export in sleazy imitation of well-known brands. Even while those guns were gaining a bad reputation in the world market, there were better guns made in Spain for use by local shooters, but foreign sportsmen did not hear of them.

To some extent the same thing has happened in Belgium, where Liege has long been one of the world's great manufacturing centers for guns. Shooters examining the immaculate Francotte double rifles and shotguns may recall some of the cheap Belgian products of a generation ago.

The term "cottage industry," often applied to gunmaking, means simply that gun parts are fashioned in individual homes and then assembled under established names of the trade. Thus, some European towns are known almost entirely as gun centers. Quality control is sometimes precarious, both as to workmanship and metals, and a propsective buyer, seeing only the exterior of an expensive gun, must rely on the reputation of a trade name.

It was the changing fortunes of labor that drove an immeasurable segment of the firearms industry to Japan. Most of the exodus was in the field of upper-middle-priced guns, both rifles and shotguns. Most major American manufacturers dealt with Japan, the Made in Japan inscription cut along with the name of the American firm.

Browning guns, mostly related to the original inventions of John Browning, had long been made by Fabrique Nationale Herstal (FN) of Liege, the world's largest maker of firearms. Increasing labor costs, however, brought on a crisis. Brownings, especially the Superposed, an over-under shotgun of high quality, have appeared in highly decorated models and some of the prices were in the upper bracket. Some eighty percent of Browning sales were in America, where the company was based. When the Belgian franc appreciated against the American dollar, European production was not feasible.

FN had sole European rights to the Browning inventions and Browning had sole U.S. distribution rights to FN guns. After heavy losses, Fabrique Nationale acquired a controlling interest in Browning and concentrated on aircraft manufacture,

193

Westley-Richards 12-gauge double (right, below) is intended especially for "live pigeon" shooting, a sport involving a great deal of money aside from cost of equipment. Like most top grade British guns, Holland & Holland (right) is in hard case with snap caps to protect firing pins in dry firing, and cleaning gear.

moving the gun construction to Japan. Now the American Browning comes from the Orient.

Ithaca, still producing a custom trap gun and a catalog of assembly-line guns in America, sells Japanese shotguns. Winchester bought part of this factory to produce over-under and side-by-side double shotguns. The Weatherby rifles, built for years by Sauer in Germany, moved to Japan and Weatherby introduced Japanese shotguns, as well.

Some Japanese names have disappeared from one brand and appeared on another, and a manufacturing concern like Miroku has made guns under a variety of trademarks. The guns made in Japan involved considerable handwork.

Most really high-priced double guns still come from Europe. The Americans lead in custom-built bolt-action rifles for big game, but a custom bolt rifle from one of the finest makers still costs only a fraction of the price of a British double. The reason is that bolt actions are largely machine-made and the custom builder handles stocking, barrel installation, and any needed alterations and decoration, whereas locks or actions of the finer doubles are almost entirely hand-fashioned along with the rest of the gun.

The fact that custom bolt-action rifles are not so expensive as the best English or Belgian double is not a reflection on the maker, simply a statement that there is somewhat less to be done in producing a fine bolt-action.

The truly modern classic rifle is a phenomenon of the period following World War II, although its general outline appeared by 1910, shortly

*Very few of the finest Italian
guns are actually produced. The
Famars name is one of the
most highly regarded, for its
mechanical quality and
decoration. Famars sidelock
shows Washington crossing the
Delaware (right). Baroque
hammers (opposite) contrast
with sculptured "fences" and
are Brancusi-like in design.
"Napoleon" gun (bottom) was
praised by Giscard d'Estaing.*

after a few sportsmen began to appreciate the qualities of the Mauser action. Although jet-age art is not confined by geography, the most of the best in current custom rifle design has come from America.

Most early custom Mausers were produced in Germany, where sporters naturally followed military designs, while Americans preferred lever-action rifles of fairly standard measurements and the English preferred doubles for heavy game. The English made a few custom bolt rifles using imported actions from Germany and Belgium. A student with the acquired taste of the gun-art lover will almost invariably consider the modern custom bolt rifle far advanced over those of seventy years ago. He will be less certain about double guns.

In addition to being the home of the Mauser, which went to many of the world's armies, Germany was a natural ground for the custom rifle. There were a great many German hunters both before and after World War I, and fine workmanship was appreciated. Except for Schuetzen arms (which first came from Germany, as had the jaeger) the enormous American market virtually ignored costly custom rifles until after World War I. Two large custom-gun firms, Griffin & Howe in New York and Hoffman Arms. Company of Cleveland, then began to produce made-to-order rifles in quantity.

Now there was strange variety in the requirements of custom-gun users. There were European rifles with superb engraving but almost total indifference to stock wood or design. The stock was merely a vehicle for fine metal engraving. In other cases there were beautiful guns with sloppy chambers and indifferent accuracy.

In America there were thousands of rifles built purely for utility, minimal conversions of crude but efficient military weapons. After both world wars there were literally millions of such actions for very little cost. It was in conversion of these actions that the American art really began, and the few masterpieces appeared along with utility arms.

Fine stocking was applied not only to military actions but to American factory bolt rifles, which began with inferior woodwork. Restocking was important when scope sights were used. After World War II there were sportsmen who insisted on custom rifles with an eye for accuracy, line, wood quality, checkering, weight, and even engraving—and were willing to pay for it.

Some rifles attained value because of their makers' names, the connoisseur able to identify the engraver or stocker instantly from his work. A new breed of engravers appeared who achieved detail and accuracy of form unapproached by the older workmen. Their skill was especially apparent in the reproduction of game animals and birds in steel or precious metals. Later engravers stressed hunting subjects rather than mythology or unrelated scenes that had been popular.

Fine stocks of any kind depend on the original wood, and walnut is the traditional material. Its desirability depends partly on its figure, or design of its grain, and partly on its strength and stability. Stability, the ability of the wood to keep its form in varying temperature and humidity, depends on grain structure and aging.

While many names are used to indicate types of walnut, two kinds are most commonly used for guns: *Juglans regia* or English walnut, and *Juglans nigra* or American black walnut. The former is likely to produce the most valuable stocks and can be expected to hold finer checkering or carving. It is grown over much of Europe and Asia and may be called French, Circassian, or Spanish, sometimes without accuracy as to its origin. Sometimes the name of the country is used deceptively to indicate a type of wood. A large share of American walnut grows in the Ozark region.

The most desirable stock wood comes from slowly grown trees in an arid climate. The growth rings are close together in such wood, thus making it more stable. English walnut grown in irrigated groves in America is likely to have wider-spaced grain and can be less stable, although somewhat lighter. Fine wood tends to be heavy.

In one description of their stocking procedures, James Purdey and Sons stated that their unshaped walnut stock blocks were aged six years

197

before delivery to the Purdey factory and five more years after that. Some of their wood had been cut thirty years before use.

In rifles accuracy may be dependent on the stability of the wood. That with "wild grain" inconsistent with the stock's design may swell, shrink, and warp, exerting pressures on the barrel and action, causing the rifle to shoot in a completely different spot after changes in humidity or through natural aging. There are many other woods used in gunstocks, ranging from spectacular maples to ornate cuttings of mesquite, but the vast majority of classic rifle and shotgun stocks are walnut.

In fitting the individual shooter, rifle stocks for hunting use are far less critical of measurement than are shotgun stocks since the rifle is aimed rather than "pointed" and the shooter can adapt more to the stock's form. But in shotgun stocks precise inletting may be chiefly for the sake of appearance while the rifle inletting has a direct bearing on accuracy. Many rifles are bedded in plastic or "glass," an efficient method which allows for some irregularity in stocking as long as room for the bedding material is allowed. Aside from all practical considerations, some shooters feel this is an avoidance of meticulous handwork, an impurity in an otherwise classic operation.

Custom-rifle builders sometimes deal with barrels and actions secured from other workmen; sometimes the builder and his staff handle all operations. A few builders do it all themselves, without an assistant. Engravers are likely to work only on that phase of the assignment, and there may be

Custom Griffin & Howe .318 Nitro Express rifle (opposite) contrasts with stark simplicity of three guns below. Parker double (left to right) made in 1934, a 20-gauge Francotte of the 1930's, and a Marlin Pumpgun of 1910. Cape Buffalos (right) show the meticulous cutting technique and are inlaid and engraved.

a barrel builder and a metalworker for action alterations. Some lovers of fine rifles actually engage the various operations separately, seeking the "best" barrelmaker, the "best" stocker, and the "best" engraver—a time- and money-consuming procedure.

But "custom" is a relative term. Most of the large manufacturers have their own shops in which standard models are decorated, smoothed, and specially stocked to varying degrees. Such guns may accept all the standard parts without alteration; the procedure is applied to both rifles and shotguns.

The true custom shotgun has some very different qualifications from those of the rifle. Whereas a rifle stock can be built to feel comfortable and serve well for shooters of a wide variety of physical characteristics, the shotgun's "fit" to the user can be as important as the rifle barrel's fit to its stock.

In fitting game guns the British have been world leaders through the "shooting school" and the "try gun." The try gun is simply a shotgun with a stock built in adjustable sections and is now used by custom builders around the world. The length, bend, castoff, pitch, and other measurements can be changed by simple adjustment, and the fitter makes it conform to the build and shooting style of the shooter. Then the customer actually shoots the gun at both stationary and moving targets to see if it follows his eye. Such measurements are used in the client's new gun and filed for future reference.

The shooting school, aside from instructing new shooters, serves as a test ground for the fitting of new guns and gives an opportunity for veterans to have their skills monitored by observant instructors. It has spread from Great Britain to dealers in custom guns elsewhere.

Many very fine shotguns are not truly "custom," although they have many of the characteristics of custom arms. In some cases commercial models are delivered with a great number of options.

One of the characteristics of the finest in over-under or side-by-side shotguns is their durability, a matter of superior fitting of the proper steels for each purpose. Since untimely wear in any part may make the gun useless and since "interchangeable" parts, if there are any, will require expert alteration, the proper steels and fitting become a major factor in its value. Since only a metallurgist with the proper equipment can judge them, the layman must rely on the builder's name.

Metalwork is more complex with shotguns than with magazine rifles, for most custom repeating rifles are made from well-known actions. Some highly decorated shotguns have disappeared from the market because they "shot loose," their bolting systems being inferior or employing improper metals. Some of the best double-gun actions are both built from proper steel and designed to absorb wear and are automatically tightened with use.

Builders of fine English shotguns may prove reticent as to the sources of their barrels, famous barrelmakers being favored by their customers. The source, of course, is unimportant if good quality steel is used, for the barrel's conformation is established at the gun factory.

This is one of the complex processes of fine shotgun making, for weight and balance become

critical. The individual gun may be ordered for a certain stated weight, a matter that must be considered with countless estimates of all the components. If additional weight is needed it cannot be added haphazardly to stock or barrel for it will interfere with balance. Stocks are hollowed or weighted as one means of regulation. Barrel length is usually preordained so thickness and taper of the barrel walls must handle that part of the weight and balance.

Some of the custom touches of fine shotguns are of minor importance in the actual shooting. Hand-filed sighting ribs can be a demonstration of great skill, although the delicate filing serves only to prevent light reflection. Shooters interested in simple utility say that any sort of stippling will do as well.

Some features become at least partly peculiar to a country or school of gunmaking. For example, single-trigger mechanisms were despised by many European makers, especially the English. Double triggers on a shotgun, they insisted, gave the shooter instant selection of barrel, whereas a selective single trigger forced extra manipulation in choosing a choke. A nonselective single trigger (much easier to make) made choke selection impossible, the same barrel firing first each time. In fine shotguns or double rifles with two triggers the forward trigger is generally hinged to prevent injury to the finger during recoil.

Critics have said the reason Europeans avoid the single trigger is simply that they have been unable to make a satisfactory one. The truth is that the single selective trigger has been a curse of gun-

Ithaca single-barrel trap guns (opposite) are still made to order with a great deal of handwork. The Ithaca custom hunting doubles have disappeared although some repeaters are engraved to order. Artistic patterns of checkering on fine wood is U.S. trademark. The classic European sidelock (left) has room for engraving. Double triggers are standard.

makers for nearly a century and has become truly reliable only recently. It must be conceded by Americans (who have led the demand for single triggers) that no other part of a high-quality gun has given so much trouble. The single trigger most often sullies the reputation of fine doubles built before 1950.

Most over-under shotguns now have single selective triggers. Nearly all the better over-under guns built in Europe, America, and Japan have them. The British prefer their side-by-side guns with double triggers and agents of British firms still advise against single triggers.

At one time it was possible to determine where a gun was made by looking at its engraving. Now, except for the work of well-known masters, it is nearly impossible. The traditional British engraving was a light scroll but now engravers will produce, on order, a variety of styles. Austrian and German engraving was very bold, usually featuring large images, often scenes from mythology. Spanish and Italian work generally fell somewhere in between. Today almost any kind of engraving can come from almost any country.

Engraving on a sideplate or action has a special purpose since long use will wear off blueing. Engraving is not disfigured by such wear, and is often somewhat enhanced by it. Custom shotguns appear with blued receivers and sideplates, with "gray" or "white" metal to hold the engraving, or with case-hardening.

There are some features which usually indicate a high-quality gun, even though they might not be noticed by the average hunter and might even be considered undesirable. The butts of some high-grade guns have no attached plate but are hand checkered. Others have skeleton buttplates or leather-covered recoil pads. Pistol-grip caps on custom rifles are often of engraved steel and rifle-bolt handles are checked or engraved. All of these features are in keeping with the conservative classic gun.

The best grades of European game shotguns tend to be somewhat lighter than mass-produced models, partly an exhibition of the craftsman's skill in achieving strength and durability without using excessive materials. For 12-gauge guns intended for maximum loads of 1¼ ounces of shot, the English side-by-side will generally range somewhat less than seven pounds and as light as six and one-half pounds while the twenty is consistently less than six pounds.

Never critical of gun weight, American upland shooters generally carry 12-gauge guns weighing well over seven pounds. There have been special models but the fine handmade guns of the American past have tended toward greater weight than those of Europe. Since nearly all American shooters except for wildfowlers do a great deal of walking and much European gunning is done from a stand, the inconsistency is difficult to justify. However, Americans of recent years have tended to use quite heavy loads, making more weight helpful for strength and recoil suppression.

In over-under guns there is less disparity, and a Purdey catalog of some years ago suggests an over-under weight of well over seven pounds in 12 gauge. The only American over-unders made in

the United States are heavier. Lighter ones are imported, even though they carry American names.

Gun weight can be reduced with lightweight alloys but custom makers hardly ever use them. Such materials vary widely in durability and although there are undoubtedly satisfactory ones they have been widely mistrusted for quality arms.

Even those ultralight guns which have proved durable have met with little success in America. An example, although not in the custom category, is the glass-barreled Winchester Model 59 semiautomatic, which was discontinued after a few years of good service. Another semiautomatic by a lesser-known firm was built of very light alloys and disappeared almost immediatcly. Perhaps the general American preference is demonstrated by a new Ruger over-under introduced in 1977 and weighing a full seven pounds in 20 gauge.

But when buying high-grade imports American connoisseurs are fond of light guns and the greatest demand is in smallbores. The 20 gauge has been greatly in demand and even the tiny .28s and .410s have been popular, despite limited game use. In some cases the little guns have become almost miniatures, and even though their basic shooting measurements are typical, the reduced actions and tiny fore ends have disadvantages for practical adult shooters. Such guns are especially attractive to collectors, commanding high prices.

Inletting is a field for showmanship on the part of the custom-shotgun maker, and the careful mating of wood to metal so it appears that "the tree grew around the steel" is a matter of pride, sometimes examined with a magnifying glass. The sidelock gun is a special showplace for the artist in wood and it displays jewellike metalwork.

Sidelock guns have their firing mechanisms installed with plates just ahead of the hand, or grip, of the stock, so opportune a place for engraving that many guns have "dummy sideplates," even though the operating parts are farther ahead and the gun is a boxlock. With meticulous handwork the locks or firing mechanisms are attached to the inner side of the plates, which are often easily removable. Some plates can be taken off by hand without so much as a screwdriver and exhibit the watchlike precision of the lockwork. The locks must be fitted into the wood of the stock and this inletting for the parts is a showplace for the carving art.

While easy removal is helpful in cleaning and repair, the interior of the lockwork can be dramatic salesmanship for expensive guns. Sometimes it is gold plated; the parts are often "jewel polished." Still, some of the more conservative makers feel flamboyant decoration might escape the bounds of utility, and keep the working parts plain.

At one extreme is the maker who does not consider the interior of the gun a part of its beauty. That, he insists, is the working part, valued solely for utility. In that department a number of fine American locks have suffered by comparison to highly polished innards of guns that were actually less serviceable. The irrefutable argument is that the appearance of working parts has nothing to do with their utility, and time and money are better spent where they really count.

There are definite schools of design in fine guns, not only with regard to engraving. The overall impression of various types, generally conveyed by stock design, is instantly cataloged by the student. Since the nonshooting public is likely to choose a firearms silhouette repugnant to the majority of collectors, the conclusion is that a taste for fine guns must be developed. Repeated tests have shown that the more flamboyant a design the more attractive it is to the nonshooting public, and even to some of the more casual gun users. The classic style has become most fashionable with expensive guns.

The "California school" commonly employs quickly distinguished features but its general characteristics have been wildly extended in rifle design. An outstanding example has been the Winslow rifles, designed in bold sweeps of line yet maintaining fine workmanship. The Winslow rifle features pistol grips extended to lengths beyond any utility and outsized cheekpieces breaking like waves over engraved stocks with large and brilliant inlays against brightly figured wood. Winslow also produces practical classic stocks on subdued pieces.

Weatherby stocks, while not quite attaining the extremes of some of the Winslow products, are best known of the California school. "Skip" checkering, a pattern of large and small wooden diamonds, has been controversial. Weatherby rifles and many rifles imported for sale under American names, have featured it. The English have largely avoided it, and it is not accepted as classic. Strangely, some of the most acclaimed stockwork has appeared on the old Schuetzen rifles in bold designs hardly adaptable

for hunting. Checkering is of minor importance for improving the grip on a gun, and some of it appears where the hand does not touch in shooting.

Checkering is judged in several ways. When the wood is capable of taking it, the masters sometimes cut it as finely as thirty lines to an inch; twenty is more common. Stock value is enhanced by sharp and even "diamonds" produced by a steady tool. When there are "runovers," or spots in which the cut has gone outside the pattern, the checkering is considered careless, and when the design is surrounded by a cut border it is sometimes discredited because the border could conceal runovers. Such is the length to which some lovers of fine guns have separated "best" from ordinary or "production" guns. Machine checkering, much improved in recent years, is quite practical. A form used on inexpensive guns and losing favor is "impressed" checkering, which is simply stamped into the wood.

Carving is often easier than high-grade checkering but when it is substituted for checkering on expensive guns it can be extremely artistic and

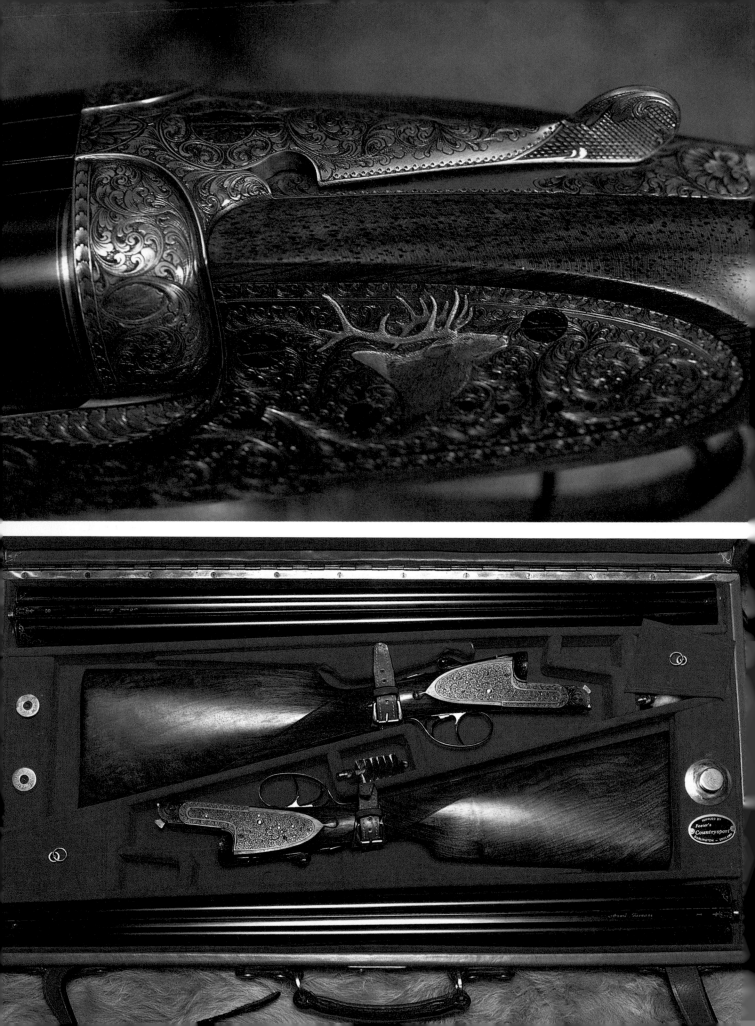

very difficult to do if there is considerable detail. Fine American checkering tends to appear in a variety of patterns, much more showy than the traditionally simple but exact English work. It is often combined with light carving.

To the despair of students of the subject, fine checkering is almost totally ignored by the uninitiated. A display of a quickly done stock carving by a high school industrial arts pupil was shown in a large gunshop beside a fine gun with checkering by a recognized master. The gun prepared by the high school lad was valued at $200 and that by the expert, obviously superior to anyone who knows guns, at several thousand. Viewers generally chose the boy's work. Checkering meant nothing to them.

Most of the fine collectors' guns were originally built for game shooting. Fine game shotguns have not changed in recent years, except for improvements in single-trigger mechanisms. It is a different story in target guns. However much they may be decorated their primary purpose is to win, so if they cannot produce trophies or money they disappear. There are some world champions who spend a great deal of money on their competition guns—for precise mechanical workmanship and the ability to fire and eject for many thousands of rounds without repair—but keep them plain.

In shotgunnery there have been a few designs that have stayed high in competition for many years, some of them considerably altered but distinctly recognizable. One is the Remington 32 over-under shotgun, which was beloved by skeet and trap shooters and disappeared in 1942 because of excessive production costs, along with other high-grade U.S. double guns.

Following World War II, the German firm of Krieghoff produced a gun similar in appearance and performance, calling it the Krieghoff 32. It was accepted happily by American competitive shooters and remains highly desired, whether in plain or ornate models, its price climbing steeply upward. It appeared in skeet sets with four pairs of barrels at prices matching those of fine automobiles and retained its popularity into the late seventies.

The Remington firm introduced its own successor to the Model 32, calling the new gun the 3200, and it too had a close resemblance to the earlier Model 32, although it featured especially fast lock time. At a much lower price than the Krieghoff, it was made largely through investment casting, which reduces handwork. All of these guns were heavy for field use.

Almost unheard of outside the world of competitive shooting are some exceptional American guns for the clay-target shooter. Ithaca's single-barrel trap gun, on special order only, has been a long-time favorite of trap enthusiasts and is still made with a great deal of painstaking handwork, usually with considerable engraving and fine wood. At the same time, Ithaca imports a number of Italian and Japanese competition shotguns.

American Ljutic guns are strangers to most field gunners and are intended solely for competition shooting in trap and skeet, largely being custom built. Although some of them are decorated, others are starkly plain tools of superb durability and

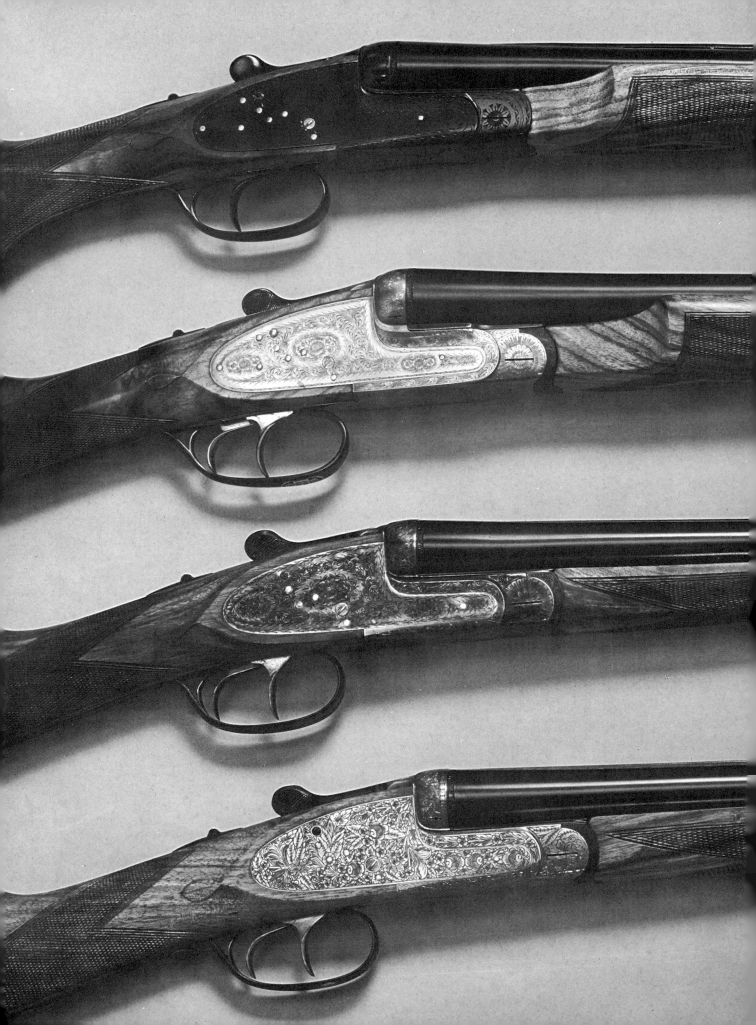

workmanship. In them there is no attempt to approximate the lines of "best" game guns. Their utilitarian form has its own beauty.

One top-grade American double, the Winchester 21, is still built on order, less costly than British guns but nevertheless expensive. It is now primarily a fine gun for the hunter since the side-by-side double has nearly disappeared from clay-target competition and is giving way to the over-under, even in live-pigeon shooting.

Demand for the Winchester 21 has kept its price high, even in the plainest grades of many years ago. Through the years the gun has varied greatly in finish and some individuals sold new for less than $80 at one time. In truth, some of those sold at high prices much later were hardly in the same class with the better models. Even in its plainest form, the gun is durable, although tending to be a bit heavy in comparison to English guns.

The oldest model in shotgun competition is the Winchester Model 12 pumpgun, and although many would abhor the thought of a "magazine gun" listed along with the world's finest, it is often engraved, stocked, and inlaid to equal them in price. Little changed since 1912, it has won more trapshooting trophies than any other gun (perhaps as many as all others combined) and is still built as a plain trap gun and in decorated grades. When it was returned to the market in a field model, some years after being discontinued because of production costs, it was not well accepted. Despite assurances by many experts, hunters would not concede that it was as good as the older Model 12. And there are trapshooters who insist the same thing about current trap models, but many are used. On special order, the high-grade Model 12 can be had in hunting models. At one time it was a leading skeet competitor but pumpguns have been largely replaced by over-unders and semiautomatics in that field.

In competitive shotgun shooting the Italian manufacturers were highly ranked in the late twentieth century, in American skeet and trap as well as in international competition. Some of their leadership is simply due to fine workmanship in that field. Originality is also a factor. One Perazzi over-under model comes with interchangeable choke tubes for both barrels, giving the trap or skeet shooter a choice of the pattern he wishes for a given situation. Some Italian competition guns also feature quickly interchangeable trigger units enabling a shooter to use the simpler nonselective single trigger and still fire the barrel he chooses in a given event.

Gun collecting had an unpredictable effect on gun values and grew rapidly in the late twentieth century. Collections have a wide variety of bases. Specialization causes some cheap guns of many years ago to become valuable through scarcity. Other collections concentrate on workmanship and some are based on the output of a single manufacturer. In addition to specialized collectors, there are a great many shoppers who hope that what they find will be of value to some collector who is seeking that particular piece. Thousands of gun owners have begun investigations to find just what their possessions were worth. Popularity of gun collecting continued to increase in the 1970s.

10

Changing Game

The rendezvous site was well chosen where Indian trails once converged in a valley, trails that were used for hundreds of years. The mountain men's tents were scattered along the bright creek and near the pines. The mountain shadows struck them early. The little valley might have been a rendezvous point for Indians before the mountain men began to use it. This was not the first meeting for the men in buckskin. Many of them were old friends, and as they began to gather in late afternoon they clustered in little groups where a tent was being set up or a fire built. At dusk there were groups around the larger fires and the visitors were noisy. There were no sentries, for the Indians had been at peace for some time.

The mountain man's life centered around his guns and much of the talk was of guns and shooting. Shooting matches were the main events of the next morning and the smell of black powder mingled all day with that of the cooking fires. Most of the events involved cap-and-ball rifles but there were a few flintlocks and pistols. The targets and scoring methods were simple and there were long discussions of proper powder charges for a given rifle, and always there was talk of trades. Some of the trading seemed to be for the sake of that game, a sort of social amenity, and there were merchants with goods to sell.

The merchants set up displays of firearms and accessories, clothing, and many other odds and ends about their camps and talked incessantly with men in soiled buckskins who wandered over from the target range or the tomahawk-throwing contest. The buckskins and big hats smelled strongly of woodsmoke and powder, and some of them had a patina acquired through long, hard usage.

But this rendezvous was different from earlier ones for this time there were no furs to sell, and when the buckskinners finished their target matches and visiting they promised to see each other the next year and carried their camping equipment up a trail to where their automobiles were parked. In the 1970s there may have been more in attendance at this meeting than there had been at a similar one one hundred and fifty years before.

A major part of twentieth-century shooting and its firearms industry is the phenomenon of thousands of American outdoorsmen who have turned to the shooting ways of yesteryear. It is a process which took some firearms builders by surprise and which has made a quiet invasion.

In a way, the costumes of muzzleloading days are a form of grownup play, yet there is more to it than nostalgia. There is some serious return to the ways of a simpler time. While most users of primitive weapons step from their twentieth-century roles for only hours at a time, there are others who spend as much of their lives as possible in the clothing and customs of the mountain men or the long riflemen.

While there have always been a few students of primitive hunting who have used old guns and collected them, the rush to black powder, muzzleloading, and flintlocks really began with the replica industry. When genuine old guns became

Waterfowlers treasure the moments of preparation in spectacular settings, even though bag limits are much restricted and gunners have wrestled with steel shot regulations. Pre-dawn setting out of decoys (preceding pages) is necessary as ducks become active at sunrise. This time affords greatest opportunity for success for the waterfowler.

scarce and expensive a few craftsmen began to build new ones in the old designs. Then came large, modern factories and assembly-line production of "readymade antiques." The new guns looked the same and worked the same although they were improved by modern technology. They were not nearly so expensive as well-preserved guns that had been made more than a hundred years ago.

One of the great pushes toward the use of old guns is the primitive-weapons hunts that have become a part of most game-management programs in America. Since the user of a muzzleloading gun is somewhat handicapped in relation to modern arms, there have been special seasons set aside for use of primitive gear only. A special attraction is the premium upon woodcraft and game knowledge, and many a sportsman who is impatient when armed with a precise modern rifle is willing to hunt for weeks without success while carrying a muzzleloader that was obsolete when his grandfather was born.

"Black-powder hunts," which involve breechloaders, are somewhat harder to set up than muzzleloader seasons, for the black-powder cartridge gun is so close to modern firearms in efficiency that it falls into a rather special category. The combination of archery seasons with muzzleloaders has proved satisfactory.

Except for modern materials most of the current primitive rifles and shotguns are in direct imitation of models of long ago. Their prices are roughly the same as those of modern guns. But as was bound to happen, for better or for worse, there is a new class of "primitive" rifles. As there were

special target models in the days of the mountain men there are now percussion rifles with adjustable weights or stocks resembling Schuetzen or free rifles. There are even "primitive" benchrest rifles.

For many years there had been costume shoots and historical pageants involving military uniforms of a bygone time, especially in reenactments of battles or skirmishes of the Civil War, but the "mountain man" image of the muzzleloading days has even wider appeal than that of the uniformed soldier. The ragtag costumes now worn at a rendezvous are somewhat removed from the spic-and-span dress costumes just a few years back, and it is likely they are more nearly what the original trappers wore. And a pair of leather leggings worn with a wide-brimmed black hat and an eagle's feather no longer attracts attention in a gunshop.

Some of the readymade collector's items have copied guns made far more recently than the muzzleloaders; others have been commemorative models of current popular American guns. Commemorative issues, generally in limited numbers, have been produced for a long list of historical reasons, such as the admission of various states to the Union. When such guns sold well the builders found an endless number of persons, places, and events to be commemorated.

Despite the opinions of many firearms experts, the guns appreciated rapidly in value and it became desirable—and expensive—to have guns with consecutive serial numbers. Some disappeared for only a few years to appear for resale, unfired and in their original cartons, at much more than their

217

Nostalgia has brought its own color to American gun lovers. Muzzleloader users (far left and left) appear in fitting costumes for shooting matches. "Ready-made antiques" of recent years are exemplified by the Roosevelt Commemorative Winchester 94 rifle (bottom, front). Plain model in saddle gun (bottom, back) is best known of "Western" repeaters.

original selling price. Some were of special quality and others were no different from guns sold for the everyday trade, but many of them would not be fired anyway.

Manufacturers probe endlessly for firearms advancements that might open new sales, sometimes aided and sometimes hindered by tradition. Millions of rifles with a deliberately fashioned resemblance to those of an earlier day have been sold to active hunters. Fashions in gun appearance have become so inflexible that rows of other new rifles would be indistinguishable from the Winchester 94 at first glance.

In some cases such new guns are built in new calibers, although that has proved a rocky road. Some of the new calibers have failed, even though obviously ballistically improved over the old. The full-magazine deer rifles have generally used cartridges of the .30-30 class but since many hunters of brush-loving whitetail deer have shown preference for heavier bullets, there have been moves in that direction.

Marlin produced a new 444 cartridge for heavy duty in the brush and Winchester designed the 375 Winchester (not the 375 H. & H. Magnum, a much more powerful load), both appearing in lever-action rifles and both using heavy bullets, believed by some to be safer in settled communities since their maximum range is less than that of flatter-shooting loads.

Some of the imported lever-action rifles that resembled the "Guns That Won the West" were chambered for pistol cartridges. The old .44-40 (used

at one time for both rifle and pistol) was popular and there were even rifles in 38 Special, a venerable pistol caliber. Most were marginally useful for deer. Others did not fill the requirements at all. And of course the ubiquitous .22 Long Rifle cartridge was used in many such rifles.

Although it had long been believed that the bolt-action rifle, whether singleshot or repeater, was potentially the most accurate of all, there was a new demand for fine falling-block singleshot rifles in the 1970s. Except for a few .22 match rifles, such as the BSA Martini of England, the falling-block action had been fading into antiquity, but the new surge to nostalgia and the ''fine old rifles of yesteryear'' revived it.

Of course, it had been the basis of the old Sharps, the Sharps-Borchardt, the Remington rolling block, the earlier Stevens target smallbores, the early Winchester singleshots (John Browning invented the Winchester that went into production in 1885), and the blackpowder Marlin Ballard. There remained some demand for such actions as the Win-

chester, which was used in varmint rifles up through World War II. The most admired was the British Farquharson, used by some of the world's finest gunmakers. The Farquharson was capable of handling big African cartridges, and such singleshots had been much less expensive than double rifles.

Sturm, Ruger & Company introduced a singleshot that was virtually a duplicate of the Farquharson in appearance and could handle cartridges ranging from light varmint rounds to the big .458. As in the case of other Ruger guns, its traditional outlines concealed highly advanced mechanical features. The firm has specialized in producing modern firearms with the same appearance as old favorites.

Not long after World War II William Ruger's concern had turned out a Ruger semiautomatic .22 pistol that so much resembled the German Luger in outward silhouette that cynical pistol hunters and target shooters guessed the design was merely a play on the Luger's famous name. But the Ruger, with some modification, became a leading target pistol.

220

America is the land of the repeater. Highly successful models of recent years are the Browning autoloader (top, opposite) and the Remington Model 760 pump (below, opposite). Even casual sportsmen can detect the grace of the lineup of shotguns at lower right. They are expensive, but top performance justifies price.

Then Ruger made a modern line of single-action revolvers with the silhouette of the old Colt Peacemaker but with completely different and highly modern mechanisms. The Ruger single-action became a favorite of hunters and could handle the big 44 Magnum cartridge, which has killed all of America's big game. After Ruger's step numerous other companies produced single-action "frontier" types of pistols and Colt went back in business with their old original.

Ruger introduced a bolt-action big-game repeater with features heretofore found mainly in the work of classic builders of custom rifles. All of the Rugers were moderately priced and fairly plain, appealing both to practicality and nostalgia.

Then came Ruger's singleshot, and although it was hard to give concrete proof that it could compete with a bolt-action repeater in efficiency, there was great demand for it. It was not especially expensive and it showed good workmanship. There were many serious hunters who now explained how they learned to carry an extra cartridge in their fore-end hand and could reload at high speed in an emergency. It was simply a rifle that many shooters wanted, even though its general design was the one from which the lever-action repeater had once been triumphantly produced, to give way before the bolt and the semiautomatic.

Then in addition to new "antique" black-powder singleshots came a Japanese-made Browning singleshot for big-game cartridges. It resembled the old Winchesters and Stevens rifles, a Wickliffe falling block in that same silhouette and a

221

Hyper-Single in the Farquharson form at premium prices. The singleshot big-game rifle was back again, apparently to stay. And, of course, there were hosts of .22 rimfire rifles made in different parts of the world as near-duplicates of American models long considered obsolete.

Making the same case as the archer and the muzzleloader shooter, the singleshot user reported that it was more sportsmanlike to hunt with the handicap of only one cartridge. The only and seldom-mentioned argument against it was the thought that a quick follow-up shot might avoid the escape of wounded game. Businesslike shooters with no regard for traditional appearance began to buy gas-operated semiautomatics shortly after World War II. In shotguns it was the Remington Model 1100 that grasped a lion's share of the market, both in hunting and clay-target shooting.

Like most semiautomatics, the Remington's handwork was minimal; so was that on the twinlike guns made by other builders. When the semiautomatics broke down they were easily repaired and the trap or skeet shooter who fired in many tournaments every year often carried a small collection of inexpensive parts he could install himself.

The main reasons the tournament shotgunner used semiautomatics, it was said, was that they gave little effect of recoil, and there were many shooters who could simply make better scores with them. It was the same type of allegiance that kept the Model 12 Winchester a leader on trap fields.

Most of the semiautomatics were rather heavy, and even when they were capable of holding only three cartridges they were snubbed in some circles, such as the formal game shoots of Europe or the quail plantations of the southern United States.

Semiautomatic big-game rifles were used for many years by deer hunters, especially in the East and South, but they had never been considered accurate enough to compete with the bolt ac-

Made in Japan, Winchester
101 Pigeon Grade 12 gauge
(opposite) is a middle-priced
venture into "dressed-up"
shotguns. Popularity of the
over-under has increased
rapidly among Americans.
Duck and goose calling (left)
has become a valued art in
days of reduced limits and
shrinking hunting areas.
Mallards (below) are the
favorite American waterfowl.

tion. This was true with carefully tuned bolt guns, but off-the-shelf semiautomatics such as the recent Browning can sometimes outshoot the factory bolt rifle. It occasionally happened with other self-loading models. Remington was the leader in quantity production after World War II and the Remingtons in field grade were less expensive than the Browning.

There were some completely new features in guns of the late twentieth century. One that failed to attract was the use of various colors in an appeal to the "decorator instincts" of women shooters. The result was that women shooters, like men shooters, preferred guns that "looked like guns." Tradition would not be moved.

It became increasingly clear that wood might not be the ideal material for gunstocks. Wood warped, shrank, and swelled, and plastic made an appearance on low-priced guns. However efficient it was, serious gun lovers rejected it for the most part. The benchrest shooters, however, preferred utility over appearance. A few big-game hunters had plastic stocks built to reduce rifle weight and found it efficient, if hardly an object of pride in their gun cabinets, even though such custom work might be more expensive than wooden stocks.

There was a similar problem with laminated wood. Careful lamination did away with nearly all the common practical faults of wood stocking and for a time a zebra pattern of colorful wood was desired. It never crowded more conservative patterns except for target shooting. There were "artificial" colorings for wooden stocks, the Japanese developing a "painted pattern" hard to tell from an

223

originally attractive wood grain. Connoisseurs who were not quite sure it was not natural at first tended to condemn it when they learned it was manmade.

In the field of decoration there were etched scenes to take the place of hand or machine engraving and the French concern, Manufrance, builders of repeating shotguns, adorned receivers with baked enamel inlays combined with rolled engraving in a variety of colors.

Ultralight shotguns made of new materials did not fare particularly well, however smoothly they performed. An unusual example is the light-alloy over-under Bretton, which may weigh as little as 4½ pounds in 12 gauge and which is feared for its potential recoil but is efficient where light loads are carried for long distances in difficult terrain.

The French, ever noted for the experimental and the unconventional, have led in the development of electrically discharged guns, meaning a simplification of firing mechanisms. Electrically fired guns virtually eliminate lock time, a long-time enemy of designers.

Although it is the French builders who persistently endeavor to circumvent the design problems of the conventional break-action, double-barreled gun, their products, however efficient, have never been widely accepted. There were reports on them in the 1970s but those French guns that found their way to the world markets were more conventional—except for the Darne with its sliding breech mechanism, and it was something of a rarity.

Telescopic sights, having gained durability and reliable adjustments, became standard equipment with big-game rifles and new scope features were stressed in the seventies. The variable-power sight improved in quality and was accepted after a period of questionable reliability. As it became more compact and rugged, a rifleman was able to change his magnification from wide angle and low magnification in heavy timber to more definition for long shots.

The traditional crosshairs were supplemented by a bold post reticle for poor light, as well as a variety of other reticles, some of which were made to aid in estimates of range. Then came the scopes with built-in elevation corrections for known ranges and it appeared that "Kentucky elevation" was to disappear for the best-equipped hunters.

Pistol hunting had a stormy career. Handguns for big game had been available since the 357 Magnum was introduced by Winchester and Smith & Wesson in 1935, and in 1955 the big 44 Magnum was introduced by Smith & Wesson with Remington. As the most powerful of factory pistol cartridges it was used with heavy-framed revolvers and later with semiautomatics.

Just as handgun shooting was gaining popularity and the telescopic sight for handguns became practical, there was a setback due to antigun movements; handgun hunting was hampered by inconsistent game laws. The pistol suffered from its reputation as a combat weapon.

Some states prohibited the possession of handguns by big-game hunters. Few countries other than the United States allowed any form of handgun hunting. The actual hunting laws in the

225

Transportation has become a major part of big-game hunting. Snowmobiles (far right) take hunters to high country and bush (opposite, left) planes give quick access to wilderness. But canoe (opposite, right), with the addition of outboard motor still brings in moose trophies. Polar bear (right) has been crowded and its hunting has been curtailed.

United States were complicated by conflicting regulations regarding the transportation of handguns in private or public conveyances. At the same time there were liberalized regulations concerning primitive guns, making muzzleloading rifles a much simpler hobby.

For half a century there was a lull in the practice of handloading. After the commercial ammunition builders perfected self-contained cartridges there was a feeling that homemade ammunition was in competition with readymade products. It was also popularly believed that handling any kind of explosives was dangerous.

In the early days of cartridges most shotgun shooters loaded their own but when shotgunners moved away from the practice shortly after 1900 it was the rifleman who led a revival of handloading. Varmint shooters and wildcatters were intrigued by the fact that they could not only produce satisfactory ammunition but in many cases could secure better performance than was available with factory ammunition.

As was the case with the buffalo hunter and his black-powder cartridges, the modern shooter found that certain combinations of components could improve his accuracy and killing power. Every rifle was a little different.

But for most shooters, handloading was an economy measure, a box of rifle ammunition being available at a fraction of its over-the-counter cost. Many who had not studied the procedures in great detail and had no thought of surpassing the quality of factory loads used their handloads for

practice and bought what they used for game. And years of handloading proved it was not dangerous at all.

Finally the large manufacturers not only made components available but began to push their sale, realizing a shooter who had the added interest of handloading would be a better customer in the long run.

Handloading was an enormous boost to trap and skeet shooting. Reloading tools were offered at a wide range of costs and some of them enabled a single operator to produce several hundred cartridges an hour. In shotgun ammunition the reloader's cost was roughly half what it would be if he bought his ammunition readymade.

The one-piece, plastic-sleeved wad was a help because it simplified cartridge construction. A few shotgunners took great pains to secure special results from a given gun, but the great majority reloaded purely for economy and confessed their product did not have quite the consistency of "factory."

In most of the world gun ownership and use has been controlled more strictly than in the United States. Americans are the traditional nation of gun lovers and the numbers of privately owned arms are uncountable. Even students of the subject vary wildly in their estimates of the numbers.

Open hunting has been continually reduced by enlarged park systems and closures on the part of land owners. Hunting leases became an out for the land owner and for the sportsmen who could afford them. The American system moved closer and closer to that of Europe. And the commercial hunting

Mountain hunting is generally
hard hunting and when a hunter
(below) has located his trophy
with modern optics, he is
likely to depend on boot
leather to reach it. The
horse packtrain (opposite,
above) is still the only
practical access to much high
hunting country. On mountain
rivers (opposite, below), big-
game hunters can sometimes
travel with "whitewater boats."

preserve fought for survival, a highly technical business, much more complex than it appeared from afar.

In principle the hunting preserve is simple. It involves the use of game raised as a crop and released for the use of hunters who pay fees to hunt. In structure it has ranged from small plots of land with hardly any accommodations for clients to palatial clubhouses presiding over large plantations or ranches. In quality, the variety of hunting is almost as great.

Small preserves close to large population centers have suffered high mortality. The game provided was generally quail, pheasants, and chukars, the latter adapting easily to semidomestic production although showing few of the characteristics of wild chukars. Quail can be raised in fairly small pens and pheasants are noted for quick reversal to a wild state once they are released from captivity.

Expenses at preserves cannot be easily estimated, though the costs of rentable guns and hunting dogs are not too difficult to measure. The perpetually unknown quantity is the cost of the game itself, and its price rises dramatically as the quality of hunting increases.

It is possible to raise bobwhite quail that are as tame as barnyard chickens, but if they are to perform like wild birds they become very expensive and must be raised in pens where they learn to fly strongly and have no direct contact with attendants. In any event the small game preserve's profits are tied closely to the percentage of game harvested. The production of an expensive bird is a waste if the shooter does not bag it, since few released birds sur-

vive to another season. The more sporting the hunt, the more expensive the birds and the more that are never bagged.

Most of the smaller preserves are found in the East and the Southeast and their rate of failure showed that preserve hunting must be expensive to pay its way. Promoters faced the fact that there can be no low-priced preserve hunting and many of the most successful preserves charge fees comparable to those of lion hunting in Africa. In the Southwest, especially Texas, there is a special form of big-game hunting in large acreages. The game can be imported exotics or American natives in various stages of "wildness." The hunter pays for the game, guide services, and transportation, and he hunts on what is, in effect, an enormous preserve.

All of the preserve concepts are closely tied to the firearms business. In fact, firearms companies are deep into the projects. There is no such thing as a "preserve" gun. The ones used are exactly the same as those made for wild game. Many young hunters get their start on preserves of one kind or another; some shooters contemplate hunting nowhere else. They save time and, in the long run, money, and have a hunting experience with the amount of effort they wish to expend.

American waterfowl hunters, who had spent a great deal of money to maintain flights from Canada, both in special taxes and in donations to Ducks Unlimited, were confronted by a new problem with studies of lead poisoning.

There was no doubt that lead pellets eaten by ducks or geese from the bottoms of marshes could cause sickness and death but the actual size of the annual loss was in dispute. Some marshes had been shot over for more than a hundred years, the resultant accumulation of spent lead pellets making it simple for waterfowl to scoop up considerable quantities during feeding. Mixed with some diets in particular the lead became a killing poison and the ammunition makers sought a material that would not harm waterfowl when eaten. Soft steel seemed the nearest to a solution but it did not have the range and penetration of heavier lead, it was very expensive, and it caused extra wear and tear to guns.

The harder steel barrels could handle the new shot but the barrels of some of the fine older guns could be damaged easily. Since the lighter-weight steel pellets were far less efficient at waterfowl ranges, some manufacturers and the National Rifle Association insisted the extra loss through crippling would offset the advantages of steel.

And there was the idea of local control, steel shot to be required only in areas where conditions were favorable to ingestion of shot and in spots where there had been loss of birds due to lead poisoning. In fact, local control was employed early in the game but the "regulated" areas were scheduled for steady increase in numbers and size.

There were some hunters who abandoned waterfowl hunting with the coming of steel shot. Others felt that the shortened ranges might actually help waterfowl numbers because the common hunter's fault of overrange shooting could be tempered by necessity. Harder steel shot did produce better patterns for as far as it was effective because

Only the shooter is familiar with a view of his opened and loaded double. It is the first sight he sees as he prepares to shoot and the last image of an ending day as he removes unfired shells.

it did not deform in the bore as much as lead shot.

Some firearms authorities announced frankly that soft steel shot was the coming ammunition and that manufacturers and shooters should accept it and make the best of it. An insistence on the old ways, they said, would play into the hands of antihunting groups. In any event, the waterfowl's best friend is the hunter and the end of waterfowl hunting might well be the end of waterfowl in America. It was drainage of marshes that had endangered ducks and geese in the first place and it was the sportsman's dollars that had arrested the wholesale destruction.

It is commonly said that there can never again be the great game shooters of the days of the commercial gunners. Reduced limits and hunting opportunity can never give hunters the chances at unlimited waterfowl in North America but there are still times and places where game is seemingly endless and there are no bag limits.

Some such shooting is enjoyed on mainland Europe and on the British Isles, although it is the property of a chosen few who can afford it. But there still remains moderately priced shooting with the bag limited only by the amount of ammunition the shooter is willing to expend and the length of time he is able to shoot. Such gunning is had in Central and South America on mourning and white-winged doves.

At the entrance of a Honduras hotel the party of gunners board a bus which will take them to their morning shooting grounds. Just before dawn the streets are almost empty and it is still dark when the bus and the truck that follows it pull to a field bordered by large trees.

The truck disgorges its cargo of youthful *secretarios* who will pick up birds for the gunners, and a shooter feels a tug at his trousers leg and looks down to see little but the gleaming teeth of his grinning assistant, a boy who has unerringly found him in the crowd. With the boy carrying his folding stool and load of ammunition the gunner chooses a spot with his back to a tree, his outline and that of his small friend broken by the trunk and brushy ground cover.

The whitewings and mourning doves begin to pass before the sun is up and the shots of the party sound like an infantry skirmish. In lulls the efficient *secretarios* dart through weeds and brush to find the fallen birds; the pile beside the shooter's stool grows rapidly.

If he can kill a bird for three shots he will be doing well and if he can average one for two he will feel it is a good day. The *secretario* keeps count, dove numbers being conveyed in the few English words he knows. A hundred birds will make a very good shoot and the farmers will be thankful for the protection of their crops and for the birds to eat in part payment for use of their land.

When the morning's shoot has ended it is very hot and the shooter watches an ox cart follow a winding trail up the side of a little mountain, the plenitude of game somehow related to a primitive way of life. To find the shooting of a hundred years ago the gunner can still move back in time and roar home again after a long weekend.

231

Typical Shotshell Charges

Gauge	Case Length inches	Shot Charge ounces	Velocity (fps)
10	3½	2	1300
10	2⅞	1⅞	1250
12	3	1⅞	1300
12	2¾	1½	1220
12	2¾	1¼	1240
12	2¾	1⅛	1300
16	2¾	1¼	1150
16	2¾	1⅛	1230
16	2¾	1	1225
20	3	1¼	1250
20	2¾	1⅛	1180
20	2¾	1	1125
20	2¾	⅞	1175
28	2¾	¾	1150
.410	3	11/16	1165
.410	3	¾	1220
.410	2½	½	1275

Center-Fire Rifle Cartridges

Cartridge	Bullet Wt. Grs.	Velocity (fps) Muzzle	Energy (ft.llbs.) Muzzle	300-yard Trajectory
17 Remington	25	4020	900	—
218 Bee	46	2860	835	11.5
22 Hornet	45	2690	720	13.0
222 Remington	50	3200	1140	7.0
222 Remington Magnum	55	3300	1330	6.1
223 Remington	55	3300	1330	5.4
22-250 Remington	55	3810	1770	4.4
225 Winchester	55	3650	1630	4.8
243 Winchester	100	3070	2090	5.5
6mm Remington	100	3190	2260	5.1
244 Remington	90	3200	2050	5.5
25-06 Remington	87	3500	2370	—
25-06 Remington	120	3120	2590	—
25-20 Winchester	86	1460	405	32.0
25-35 Winchester	117	2300	1370	12.5
250 Savage	100	2820	1760	7.4
256 Winchester Magnum	60	2800	1040	12.0
257 Roberts	100	2900	1870	7.0
6.5mm Remington Magnum	120	3030	2450	5.7
264 Winchester Magnum	100	3700	3040	4.2
264 Winchester Magnum	140	3200	3180	4.9
270 Winchester	130	3140	2850	5.3
270 Winchester	150	2800	2610	7.6
280 Remington	150	2900	2800	6.1
284 Winchester	150	2900	2800	6.3
7mm Mauser	139	2710	2280	7.8
7mm Mauser	175	2490	2410	9.5
7mm Remington Magnum	150	3260	3540	4.9
30 Carbine	110	1980	950	21.7
30-30 Winchester	150	2410	1930	12.5
30 Remington	170	2120	1700	14.0
30-06 Springfield	150	2970	2930	6.0
30-06 Springfield	180	2700	2910	8.3
30-06 Springfield	220	2410	2830	9.8
30-40 Krag	180	2470	2440	9.9
300 Winchester Magnum	180	3070	3770	5.3
300 H&H Magnum	180	2920	3400	5.8

continued above

Cartridge	Bullet Wt. Grs.	Velocity (fps) Muzzle	Energy (ft./lbs.) Muzzle	300-yard Trajectory
300 Savage	150	2670	2370	9.3
303 Savage	180	2140	1830	14.0
303 British	180	2540	2580	8.2
308 Winchester	150	2860	2730	7.0
308 Winchester	180	2610	2720	8.9
32 Winchester Special	170	2280	1960	12.5
32 Remington	170	2120	1700	13.0
32-20 Winchester	100	1290	370	38.0
8mm Mauser	170	2570	2490	10.5
338 Winchester Magnum	200	3000	4000	6.0
348 Winchester	200	2530	2840	4.7
35 Remington	150	2400	1920	13.0
350 Remington Magnum	200	2710	3260	—
351 Winchester Self-Loading	180	1850	1370	21.5
358 Winchester	200	2530	2840	9.4
375 H&H Magnum	300	2550	4330	8.3
38-40 Winchester	180	1330	705	36.5
44 Magnum	240	1750	1630	26.0
444 Marlin	240	2400	3070	—
44-40 Winchester	200	1310	760	36.5
45-70 Government	405	1320	1570	32.5
458 Winchester Magnum	500	2130	5040	12.0

Weatherby Magnum Cartridges

Cartridge	Bullet Wt. Grs.	Velocity (fps) Muzzle	Energy (ft./lbs.) Muzzle	300-yard Trajectory
224 Weatherby Varmintmaster	50	3750	1562	9.0
240 Weatherby	90	3500	2444	4.5
247 Weatherby	100	2555	2802	4.4
270 Weatherby	130	3375	3283	4.5
270 Weatherby	150	3245	3501	5.0
7mm Weatherby	154	3160	3406	5.0
300 Weatherby	180	3245	4201	5.2
340 Weatherby	250	2850	4510	6.7
378 Weatherby	270	3180	6051	5.2
460 Weatherby	500	2700	8095	10.0

Representative Black-Powder Cartridges

Caliber	Bullet Weight gr.	Muzzle Velocity (fps)
.32-20	115	1250
.32-40 Marlin & Winchester	165	1450
.38-45 Ballard	190	1380
.40-50 Sharps & Remington	265	1410
.40-90	370	1385
.44 Henry	200	1150
.45-90	300	1554
.45-70	400	1044
.500/.450 Musket	480	1300

Representative Muzzle-Loading Charges

Caliber	Ball Diameter Ins.	Muzzle Velocity fps.
.58 Civil War Rifle, U.S.	.570-.575	948
.577 Enfield Rifle	.570-.575	925
.54 Halls Carbine	.535	1360

*Black powder ballistics
courtesy Hodgdon Powder Co., Inc.*

Picture Credits

AdZ—Arie de Zanger
RJK—Robert J. Kligge
NYPL—New York Public Library
JBO—J. Barry O'Rourke
RAC—Remington Arms Company
WGM—Winchester Gun Museum

We wish to thank the following for lending equipment for photographs:
The Crossroads of Sport, Inc., 5 East 47th Street, New York, New York;
Thatcher Foxglove Gallery, 1050 Second Avenue, New York, New York;
Funchies, Bunkers, Gaks and Gleeks, 1050 Second Avenue, New York, New York;
F. Gorevic & Son, Inc., 660 Lexington Avenue, New York, New York;
The Guv'nor & Mrs. A, 1050 Second Avenue, New York, New York.

Bibliography

Bauer; (top rt) Leonard Lee Rue III; 170: Fred Breummer; 171: Erwin A. Bauer; 172: Bill McRae.

8. Precision and Perfection
174–175: Charles F. Waterman; 178: (top) AdZ; (btm) Charles F. Waterman; 179: Tom Brakefield; 180: JBO; 181: Bob Stahlman; 182: Dick Anderson; 183: (top) RAC; (btm) Dick Anderson; 184: Dick Anderson; 185: Robert Elman; 186–187: RJK; 188: Charles F. Waterman

9. For the Chosen Few
190–191: RJK; 194–195: JBO; 196: Roger Barlow; 197: Roger Barlow; 198–199: RJK; 200: AdZ; 201: (top) AdZ; (btm) JBO; 202–203: JBO; 204: Ithaca Gun Company; 205: Charles F. Waterman; 206–207: (top) Weatherby, Inc.; (btm) JBO; 209: Roger Barlow; 210: (top) JBO; (btm) RJK; 211: JBO; 212: Orvis Gun Company.

10. Changing Game
214–215: Paul McLain; 218–219: Charles F. Waterman; 219: Russ Carpenter; 220: AdZ; 221: Peter Miller; 222: Charles F. Waterman; 223: (top) Russell Tinsley; (btm) Erwin A. Bauer; 224: Charles F. Waterman; 225: Sil Strung; 226: Steve McCutcheon; 227: (top) Charles J. Farmer; (btm left) Tom Brakefield; (btm rt) Paul McLain; 228: Tom Brakefield; 229: (top) Tom Brakefield; (btm) Charles J. Farmer; 230: Peter Miller

Askins, Col. Charles. *The Shotgunner's Book.* Harrisburg, Pennsylvania: Stackpole Books, 1958.

Bearse, Ray. *Sporting Arms of the World.* New York: Harper & Row, 1976.

Bogardus, A. H. *Field, Cover and Trap Shooting.* New York: Forest & Stream, 1891.

Brander, Michael. *Hunting and Shooting.* New York: G. P. Putnam's Sons, 1971.

Bristler, Bob. *Shotgunning, the Art and the Science.* New York: Winchester Press, 1976.

Camp, Raymond R., ed., *The Hunter's Encyclopedia.* Harrisburg, Pa.: The Telegraph Press, 1948.

Carmichel, Jim. *The Modern Rifle.* New York: Winchester Press, 1975.

Gard, Wayne. *The Great Buffalo Hunt.* Lincoln: University of Nebraska Press, 1959.

Garwood, G. T. *Gough Thomas's Gun Book.* New York: Winchester Press, 1970.

Greener, W. W. *The Gun and Its Development (1881).* New York: Bonanza Books.

Hagel, Bob. *Game Loads and Practical Ballistics for the American Hunter.* New York: Alfred A. Knopf, 1978.

Hinman, Bob. *The Golden Age of Shotgunning.* New York: Winchester Press, 1971.

Johnson, Peter H. *Parker, America's Finest Shotgun.* New York: Bonanza Books, 1961.

Kauffman, Henry J. *The Pennsylvania Rifle.* Harrisburg, Pennsylvania: Stackpole Books, 1960.

Lind, Ernie. *The Complete Book of Trick and Fancy Shooting.* New York: Winchester Press, 1972.

O'Connor, Jack. *The Big Game Rifle.* New York: Alfred A. Knopf, 1952.

O'Connor, Jack, and Goodwin, George G. *The Big Game Animals of North America.* New York: E. P. Dutton, 1961.

Peterson, Harold L. *Pageant of the Gun.* New York: Doubleday, 1967.

Peterson, Harold L., and Elman, Robert. *The Great Guns.* New York: Ridge Press/Grosset & Dunlap, 1971.

Roosevelt, Theodore. *African Game Trails.* New York and London: Syndicate Publishing, 1909.

Russell, Carl P. *Guns on the Early Frontiers.* New York: Bonanza Books, 1957.

Wallack, L. R. *American Shotgun Design and Performance.* New York: Winchester Press, 1977.

Waterman, Charles F., *Hunting in America.* New York: Ridge Press/Holt, Rinehart, and Winston, 1973.

Watrous, George R., Rickhoff, James C., and Hall, Thomas H. *The History of Winchester Firearms.* New York: Winchester Press, 1966.

Woolner, Frank. *Grouse and Grouse Hunting.* New York: Crown Publishers, 1970.

Index

Italic numbers refer to illustrations